THE POWER OF MIND ENGINEERING

Cyril C. George, PhD, is one of India's foremost HR leaders with over 35 years of experience in the public sector and has held top management positions in the public port sector. Dr George has been conducting in-depth research on science, spirituality, spiritual science, yoga, pranayama and meditation for over 30 years, and has delivered hundreds of spiritual training programmes for professionals, sportsmen, students and corporates with incredible results received as testimonials. Attendees of the programmes have reported drastic improvements in efficiency, reduced stress, mental wellness, healing of illnesses and pain, overcoming addictions, maximizing sports performance and a higher quality of an awakened life. Dr George has developed an approach assimilating ancient spiritual wisdom with insights of modern science called 'mind engineering' to help people achieve a higher level of awareness, wisdom, quality of life and awakening leading to fundamental transformation. He can be contacted on cyrilgeorge2002@gmail.com. For more information about his work, please visit http://www.bodymindengineering.com/

THE POWER OF MIND ENGINEERING

How to Create a Stress-Free,
Happy and Healthy Life

Cyril C. George, PhD

Published by
Rupa Publications India Pvt. Ltd 2022
7/16, Ansari Road, Daryaganj
New Delhi 110002

Sales centres:
Bengaluru Chennai
Hyderabad Jaipur Kathmandu
Kolkata Mumbai Prayagraj

Copyright © Cyril C. George 2022

The views and opinions expressed in this book are the author's own and the facts are as reported by him which have been verified to the extent possible, and the publishers are not in any way liable for the same.

All rights reserved.
No part of this publication may be reproduced, transmitted, or stored in a retrieval system, in any form or by any means, electronic, mechanical, photocopying, recording or otherwise, without the prior permission of the publisher.

P-ISBN: 978-93-5520-155-3
E-ISBN: 978-93-5520-161-4

Seventh impression 2024

10 9 8 7

The moral right of the author has been asserted.

Printed in India

This book is sold subject to the condition that it shall not, by way of trade or otherwise, be lent, resold, hired out, or otherwise circulated, without the publisher's prior consent, in any form of binding or cover other than that in which it is published.

*Dedicated to those
who believe in mind alchemy*

CONTENTS

Preface ix

1. Resistance to Change 1
2. Introspection 12
3. Basic Questions and the Goal of Life 24
4. Who Am I? 28
5. Mind Engineering Model of Mind and Consciousness 37
6. Consciousness and Presence 69
7. Origin, Growth and Operation of the Ego-Mind 85
8. Freedom from Emotional Reaction and Pain 103
9. Thoughts and Energy 126
10. Why is Meditation Essential? 144
11. Healing Power of the Mind 161
12. Reprogramming of Subconscious Mind 179
13. Why Is Practice Essential? 203
14. Accessing and Experiencing Awakening 218

Notes 239
Bibliography 260

PREFACE

This book is a product of the requests of many people who desired to have all the information on mind engineering in one place. Many of us have developed a sense of prejudice and scepticism about everything to varying degrees. Those who approach this book with an open mind, participating in the journey towards awakening with full acceptance of this new wisdom, will benefit immensely, and experience transformation, awakening and a shift in awareness. A few readers with prejudiced minds might approach the book with apprehension when they start reading; the mindset is 'let me see it', and an opinion (mostly negative) is formed quietly. This is a strategy of the ego-mind to resist change. This aspect is dealt with in detail in the book. Everybody has the freedom to have his own opinion, but a reader with a prejudiced mind may not get the desired result from the book. He may get lots of information, but the transformation, awakening and shift in awareness happen only beyond the ego-mind's prejudices.

Another point I would like to mention apologetically is that the masculine gender has been used in this book to refer to both genders only for the sake of convenience. I have equal respect for both genders, but as it is practically inconvenient to use 'he' and 'she' all the time, masculine gender has been used for convenience in representing both.

As the book's ultimate goal is to achieve and experience a state of awakening, which is a panacea for all problems, conflicts, stress, pain and ill health, we need to undertake an inward journey. Each chapter is a step or level of higher awareness in the journey towards transformation and awakening; the level of awareness to be achieved from each chapter is stated at the end of the introduction. It would help the reader move ahead step by step and achieve the ultimate goal, the awakening. I am sure an open-minded reader without a judgemental attitude will be a transformed person when he completes reading the book. As mind engineering wisdom is subtle, requiring deeper understanding and awareness, it has been explained in a lucid manner with simple examples.

As the ultimate goal of our life is to evolve spiritually to a state of awakening, this book's role is like a guide or spiritual guru to lead us to that goal or destination. So, each chapter is a step towards that destination. To put it in a metaphor, suppose a group of three people is undertaking a spiritual journey to a holy place on a hilltop for experiencing awakening by ascending a narrow path in a jungle that has many steps. It requires the guidance of a learnt guide to reach the destination. Each one in the group is offered assistance. The first person is sceptical about the benefit of the journey and refuses to go further. The second, who has undertaken the journey half-heartedly, does not complete the journey and reach the destination. The third person, though he is an ordinary man and partially blind, is open-minded. With full belief in the guide, he willingly accepts the offer, undertakes the journey with full commitment, reaches the destination and experiences the state of awakening.

Likewise, we should participate in the mind engineering process, the journey towards awakening with an open mind and commitment, and ensure that each chapter or step of awareness is fully clear, so that we become fully aware and move forward.

I am sure this book will also be immensely beneficial for therapists, counsellors as well as those who are suffering mentally.

Any thought, emotion or action that is not essentially relevant to the present moment is the ego-mind's strategy for its survival by denying us the ability to pay attention to and experience of presence.

1

RESISTANCE TO CHANGE

Medical science tells us that most illnesses result from stress, negative thoughts, emotions and poor lifestyle. We do daily exercises, yoga, meditation, take part in training programmes and read spiritual books to stay away from ill health. But in most cases, we are not able to indulge in such activities regularly and make meaningful changes in life. We are not aware of the strong force, the ego-mind that is driving us, which resists any change or improvement.

It is said that we have about 60,000 thoughts every day, out of which 70–80 per cent are negative, and more than 90 per cent are similar to those we have had in the past.[1] The subconscious mind is a default programme developed by the age of seven based on experiences and conclusions. Later in life, this ego-mind is the real driving force controlling about 95 per cent of our lives, which we are not aware of. The subconscious mind also develops a belief system, a pattern of perception and a negative emotional reaction pattern in the later part of our life. This pattern of life results in a lot of conflicts, pain and stress. This aspect of unconsciousness or darkness within us needs to be lightened up with new awareness and wisdom. As per the Upanishads, Jnana Yoga (the path of wisdom) is one of the methods for self-realization. This approach is also followed in the mind engineering process.

All spiritual and scientific wisdom tells us that there are different parts of the mind. Most accepted descriptions about the mind teach us about its two broad parts, usually referred to as the ego-mind and the true self.

The ego-mind or the emotional mind is the sum total of the self-images, roles, learnt perceptions and beliefs. The brain's left hemisphere is its main processing area and is physically much stronger than the true self. This is the dominant driving force that controls most parts of our lives. Its basic nature is pain, a sense of lack and a sense of separateness. The approach of the ego-mind is based on emotional reactions referring to either the past or the future, resulting in constant conflict and pain.

The true self or consciousness is processed mainly in the right hemisphere and the neocortex of the brain. Its approach is rational, experiential and rooted in the present. It looks at everything and everyone as interconnected and a part of one larger consciousness; its basic nature is love, peace and joy.

We are what we think. Our body and life are the manifestations of our minds. Why can't we control and manage our minds, thoughts, emotions and behaviour? We are not aware of the fact that our life is driven by our subconscious mind, which includes our beliefs and perceptions. Without us being aware, our ego-mind drives us; we are identifying with the images and roles in the ego-mind. The solution lies in bringing in more awareness, which can reprogramme our subconscious mind, and follow a lifestyle driven by this new awareness. Mind engineering is an approach aimed at achieving the goal to be free from stress, problems, mental pain and ill health, and to have a life filled with love, peace, joy, good health and wellness.

Caution! There Is Stiff Resistance to Transform

Due to suffering in life, some people feel a deep urge and the need to transform and make committed efforts to achieve the goal of leading a stress-free life, but some may be sceptical or judgemental. Many fall prey to the strategies of the ego-mind and resist change. Some readers have an attitude of 'let me see how the book is'; such people will obtain a lot of information, but will not be able to undergo the process of transformation. Those who read the book with an open mind, full commitment, practise the suggested methods and continue them until the end will benefit the most. The process of an internal journey is one that needs the help of a guide. To put it in an example, suppose the goal of a blind person (unconscious) is to reach a temple (goal) on the hilltop, for which he needs the help of somebody to move ahead step by step and reach the goal (awakening). If he is open-minded, committed and listens to the guide, he will move ahead step by step with full awareness and reach the goal. Another person, even if partially sighted, may not reach the goal if he is not willing and listening to the guide. Likewise, a fully sighted person will not reach the goal if he is sceptical and refuses to undertake the journey with an open mind.

Let us start the mind engineering process or journey towards awakening. When we undertake this journey with commitment, step by step, we automatically reach higher levels of awareness. It is like lighting small candles on every step of the path towards the destination. We need not make efforts to shed light; when the candle is lit, the shedding of light and dispelling of darkness is automatic. Likewise, we will start manifesting the changes or benefits of higher awareness at each step of awareness in our life. We will start having new, positive and healthy experiences.

When we start living a life without identifying with the ego-mind and follow a rational approach with higher mind engineering wisdom, we will experience and manifest joy, health and wellness.

The mind engineering process basically involves three aspects: higher awareness, full attention with higher awareness and 100 per cent experience of every moment and activity. These are the pillars of the mind engineering approach. The ego-mind is developed in childhood based on the experiences and conclusions drawn during that phase, which need not necessarily be the truth. In a normal case, we are not aware of this aspect of our personality that drives our lives. So, we live in a state of unconsciousness (in the spiritual context), but we need to have a clearer and deeper awareness of everything, ourselves, others, the world, the goal towards life and a new approach in life. We need to address the basic questions of life: 'What is the goal of life? Who am I? Is the material world real? Is the world linear? Why do we follow a negative pattern of thoughts, emotions, behaviour, etc.?' Higher awareness of all these vital perceptions and aspects of life will help us change our beliefs, perceptions formed in the subconscious mind and patterns of thoughts, emotions and behaviour (the programme)—this will help us transform and reach a state of awakening.

This higher awareness will help us become acquainted with the reasons behind conflicts and pain in life, and the various strategies and illusions created by our ego-mind due to which we lead a life of emotional reactions relating to the past or future. With higher awareness and certain practices, we will be able to segregate or refine the present moment or the reality from the illusory continuum of past–present–future, and gradually remain focussed in the present moment and its experiences, where there is no problem, no mental pain and suffering—this is the state of awakening.

When there is a shift in awareness in everything in life, when our life is anchored in the present moment, our quality of experience from one moment to another will be of a higher order. Our brain, mind and every cell of the body will respond positively to create good health, joy and wellness in life.

Pain, a sense of lack and a sense of separateness are the basic nature of the ego-mind, which it maintains and strengthens by creating negative emotions and identifying with false images. In short, life in the negative zone adversely affects our health and wellness. So, the ego-mind will use all our intelligence to find justifications and strategies to resist change or transformation towards the positive zone, where it fears losing its control over us. So, the ego-mind will resist any opportunity, idea, effort or initiative to change or transform into the positive zone that we should be aware of.

Managing the Resistance of Ego-Mind, the Challenging Problem

When a person becomes aware of the ego-mind's resistance to change and lives with consciousness identity, the ego-mind loses its control on us and its survival comes under question. In a later chapter, we will see various strategies that the ego-mind deploys and the illusions it creates to resist change. So when we are in the transformation process, the ego-mind is in a fight for survival. It uses all our intelligence to win the war with our true self to resist change.

Stress and Consequences

Today, everybody lives in a state of stress, irrespective of whether they are rich or poor, employed or unemployed; stress is the order of the day. Stress is associated with negative emotions, which have an adverse impact on the health of human beings. Free radicals are the most harmful molecules in the body; at higher cortisol levels (stress), excess calcium enters our brain cells and produces free radicals, which trigger many illnesses, including faster aging.[2] High cortisol also causes damage to mitochondria, resulting in fatigue.[3] It has been reported that many cancer patients have had some sort of severe negative emotional experiences, causing hurt, guilt, vengeance, ill will, etc., a few years before the detection of cancer in their body. What is the biochemistry behind this? There is a gland called the adrenal glands just above the kidneys; it normally produces the stress hormones cortisol and adrenaline. The adrenal gland is directly connected to the pituitary gland, which is the master gland regulating other glands. The pituitary gland, which is connected mainly to the hypothalamus, senses various signals and situations and sends the required signals to other glands for multiple functions depending on the nature of the situation. When there is severe stress, negative emotion, or threat to existence, they generate intense fear, which triggers the body to prepare itself for facing threatening or dangerous situations.

This information is sent to the pituitary gland, and it, in turn, sends signals to the adrenal glands to produce cortisol and adrenaline. Nature envisages that human beings need to face life-threatening situations, like ancient man faced wild animals, where two options were available for his survival: he could have run away for safety (flight) or faced the animal with strength (fight); both the options require a high levels of energy.

The cortisol and adrenaline will increase to increase the heartbeat, lead to deep and frequent breathing for more oxygen, strengthen the muscles with more blood and supply extra glucose for increased energy. As our survival mode or brainstem is fully activated, the blood from the neocortex will be squeezed and diverted to the brainstem, reducing our rational thinking ability. But in the modern era, as people identify with the ego-mind, threats to the ego-image from life situations at home, workplace or in social interactions are perceived as a threat to existence that activate the defense mechanisms and biochemical processes. When glucose and insulin levels are up for many days routinely, we develop a state of insulin resistance, which is the precursor of type 2 diabetes. It will be accompanied by hypertension, obesity, cardiovascular diseases, etc. Another unhealthy situation arising out of prolonged high sugar is the tendency to activate cancer cells. It is found that 'stress leads to increased adrenal-cortical activity and consequent deficiency of T-cells, impairment of host defense system and increased HPA axis activation.'[4] Short-term stresses from challenging situations are not much harmful to the body, but long-term stress will take a heavy toll on our health.[5]

It Is a Medical Emergency to Transform

Let us look at long-term stress more closely at the cellular level. It is a widespread belief that our genes control our biology. Recent research findings reveal that instead of genes, the environment predominantly controls and influences our cells' health.[6] A cell's life is controlled not by its genes, but mainly by the physical and energetic environment, which includes our thoughts, emotions, perceptions and belief in humans. We are all made up of about 40 trillion cells. Research suggests that our negative and stressful lifestyle has a severe impact on our health. When negative emotions, like fear, are experienced, the production of bio-chemicals of love, like dopamine, serotonin, endorphins and oxytocin, gets blocked. It also causes the release of stress hormones and inflammatory agents, which lead to a stoppage of growth and even death of cells. Medical science tells us that most illnesses are due to negative thoughts and emotions. So, stress causes an adverse impact on all aspects of health and wellness.

Thus, mind engineering wisdom is necessary to be able to become aware of the lifestyle driven by the ego-mind, its consequences and decide to reprogramme our subconscious mind to have higher awareness and experience a shift in perceptions and beliefs. This will help us lead a healthy, positive and happy life. So, we are in the midst of a medical emergency of transforming towards the positive zone.

Is There a Ray of Hope, Can We Transform?

There is a ray of hope. The most significant sign of the ray of hope is the increasing awareness among human beings about the collective madness of an ego-mind-driven life. More and more people are becoming aware of the true path of life in resonance with the frequency of the creator—the true spiritual path. Spiritual awakening is the urgent need of the hour for the conservation of the earth as well as the survival of humanity. Spiritual awakening will facilitate the 'flowering' of one's personality to its full potential and help one lead a meaningful and happy life.

A detailed study conducted by Mathew A. Harris, Caroline E. Brett and J. Deary shows that our personality traits can be totally changed or transformed over a period.[7] The study, which extended to a period of 63 years, concluded that those who take responsibility of what happens in their life can dramatically change their life to make way for positivity and health.

The Transformation Process and Awakening

Mircea Eliade's studies commented upon the Patanjali Yoga practices and referred to it as a process of systematic decommissioning of human beings, which can result in 'rebirth to a conditioned mode of being'.[8] Jesus said that everybody needs to be reborn as children to enter heaven, and the kingdom of heaven is within. The basic teaching of Buddhist practices is to identify, deconstruct and remove these mental fabrications with a view to realize nirvana or transcendence—the deconditioned ego-mind. The school of Mahayana Buddhism, founded by Nagarjuna, teaches us how to systematically decommission the beliefs and perceptions of the ego-mind to reach a state of pure consciousness called the middle way or emptiness.

A similar process is involved in the mind engineering process of transformation from the ego-mind identity to consciousness identity. Usually, the following steps are involved in the transformative process through higher awareness. Like the story of a jungle boy who was brought up by monkeys, we are not aware of who we really are. We are not aware that we are living consciousness or spiritual beings with human experiences. So, the process involves the following stages.

i. **Receipt of information:** We get information about how the subconscious mind was developed and how the ego-mind is operating and controlling our lives.
ii. **Knowledge stage:** Information is received by us as new knowledge about the mind and consciousness, that we are identified with ego-mind, and in reality, we are not the ego-mind, but consciousness.
iii. **Awareness stage:** We become increasingly aware that we are living consciousness with the help of introspection,

meditation, scientific and spiritual knowledge, higher awareness, wisdom, the experience of glimpses of consciousness and living examples of others.

iv. **Wisdom stage:** We gain the new wisdom that we are living consciousness, spiritual beings, but we practically find it difficult to shed old perceptions, beliefs, patterns of thoughts, emotions and behaviour.

v. **Experience:** We become fully aware that we are spiritual beings with human experiences. With this higher awareness, we need to practise and experience life as living consciousness. We should have a life of human experiences of manifesting pure consciousness.

Questions Before Us

So far, without awareness, we have been living in the negative zone, creating negative thoughts and emotions, and following an unhealthy lifestyle. This lifestyle produced many toxins in the body and created conflicts and pain, and we were wreaking havoc in our lives without awareness.

Now being aware of it, what do we do? Will anybody create hell for himself deliberately with awareness? If so, what do we call him? Foolish? Insane? We have seen that in society, many transformed to the positive zone and started living a successful and fulfilling life. If there is a wonderful opportunity for a person to be successful in life, and if he is not availing it, what will we call him?

You are in the same position.

The mind engineering process provides that wonderful opportunity; it is a journey towards the positive zone, transformation and awakening. Are you willing and ready without resistance?

Let us say YES and start the journey step by step. We have already taken the first step, and each subsequent chapter is one step of higher awareness towards the ultimate goal. The next step is introspection about the urgent need for transformation and the stiff resistance to change.

2

INTROSPECTION

In this modern era, we have achieved a lot in terms of scientific and technological advancements, knowledge and amenities of life. However, on the other hand, stress, conflicts and sufferings have increased and have become the order of the day. Today, though we have all the information at our fingertips, we do not have the answers to basic questions about self, life and the world, like 'Who am I?', 'What is the goal and purpose in life?', 'How do we have subjective experiences?', 'Why are we not happy most of the time?', 'Why are conflicts and stress gradually increasing at the individual and social levels despite all scientific and technological developments?', 'Shall we continue the same life pattern or change?' We need to introspect step by step, starting from the gargantuan and incomprehensible dimension of the universe.

Earth Is a Miracle Gift from the Cosmic Architect

The Cosmic Architect has provided a wonderful gift to humanity, the Earth, with abundance, blessings, fortunes, resources and opportunities to lead a happy and fulfilling life. In the cosmic realm, the vastness of the cosmos is infinite and beyond the comprehension of human intellect. Physicists have discovered that the basic feature of the cosmos is multiverse (many universes), not a singular universe as we understand it. There are billions of galaxies and solar systems, stars, planets and space bodies in the cosmos. Earth is situated in the Milky Way galaxy. The diameter of our galaxy is about 100,000 light years! Light can travel around the Earth seven times in one second. The number of stars in the universe is about 100 thousand million. Our neighboring galaxy, Andromeda, is approximately 2.5 million light years from Earth. This galaxy has about one trillion stars in it. However, there is no evidence so far about life forms existing on any of the planets in space. In the whole cosmos, the Earth has been uniquely created and positioned to support life forms. For example, carbon is essential to support life forms. Carbon was produced as a result of chemical reactions between many elements inside the stars; then, it was scattered in the universe through a supernova explosion and condensed as planets in a solar system. Stars were furnaces for creation of new planets in the universe; this process spanned across 10 billion years.

Physicists estimate the age of the universe to be 13.7 billion years. Our beautiful Earth was created roughly 4,600 million years ego through this long process and presented to human beings by the Cosmic Architect. Compared to the long gestation period of planet Earth, human beings have had a truly short history. Homo sapiens are believed to have originated only 200,000 years ago. Writing, as a form of expression, started being used only about 7,000 years back.[1]

It is astonishing to note that the Earth is created, placed, set in motion and taken care of by the Cosmic Architect with an infinite number of miraculous combinations and arrangements with careful precision to support the life system. The orbits of the planets are either circles or ellipses (squashed circles wide along one axis and narrower along another). The degree to which an ellipse is squashed by eccentricity is measured in the range zero to one, showing how close an ellipse is to a circle. The Earth's orbit with 2 per cent eccentricity is near-circular, which supports its habitable weather system. A minor variation in the eccentricity of the Earth's orbit would have boiled or frozen the oceans in different seasons. Mercury, having 20 per cent eccentricity, has a temperature variation of about 200°F. Physicists call the habitable zone of the universe 'Goldilocks zone,' where planets can have liquid water to support life systems; in our vast solar system, there is only a tiny strip of habitable zone wherein Earth has been placed.[2] If we refer to the Sun, there are many stars 100 times bigger in mass or 100 times lesser in mass. Had the Sun been bigger or lesser in mass, Earth would have become uninhabitable.

Having seen the delicate and miraculous manner in which the Earth is positioned with precision in the solar system in the universe, Isaac Newton said that the universe was 'created by God at first, and conserved by him to this day in the same state and condition.'[3] Upon monitoring the universe at a cosmic as well as microscopic level, including a cell, an atom or a DNA, one can experience an abstract form of intelligence at work. But the human intellect has limitations in unravelling all the mysteries of even an atom or the functioning of a cell. After a long journey, science concludes the unification of all forces and energy fields, i.e., all these fields arise from a primary field, a unified field of energy—the 'field' pointing towards one source of all—the Cosmic Architect or cosmic consciousness. As humanity, do we gratefully acknowledge the wonderful and precious gift of the Cosmic Architect?

Are We Doing Justice to the Precious Gift?

When we look back at the history of the human race, we can see the astonishing developments in science, technology, amenities of life, infrastructure, etc. But these developments are eclipsed by the history of misuse of developments in science and technology for destructive purposes, such as making of bombs, weapons and consequent wars. Human history is also maligned by the miseries, destruction, tortures and violence caused by man on fellow human beings. It is estimated that by the end of this century, human beings would have killed about 100 million fellow humans.[4] Politics and religions are meant to enable better living in the world, but genocides perpetrated in history by political and religious movements have killed more human beings than natural calamities.

Today, due to the stockpiling of weapons of mass destruction and increasing levels of conflicts and violence, the entire Earth and humanity are struggling to survive. The collective mind of the people is driven by fear, greed and pain. Conflict and misery are the order of the day. A sense of peace, love and joy is eroding extremely fast from the minds of the people.

Nature has provided resources in abundance for humanity to lead a happy and fulfilling life, but the resources are misused for disastrous purposes. The resources we spend on arms and ammunition in a year are more than sufficient to feed the world's entire population for a year. Nature envisages that all human beings lead a healthy, happy and fulfilling life. However, we indulge in many activities that are detrimental to nature and ourselves, resulting in destruction of forests, pollution of the environment, soil erosion, unscientific use of natural resources, depletion of the ozone layer, etc.

Are We Doing Justice to Ourselves?

Over the centuries, there has been an erosion of spiritual wisdom in human civilizations. Spiritual wisdom from Tibet and Greece, spanning thousands of years, are still invaluable treasures that the modern man is trying to interpret. Due to the erosion of spiritual wisdom in life, people have become increasingly self-centered and ego-minded, identifying with emotional mind-created images and material achievements. This has resulted in the emergence of an ego-mind-based culture of being addictively engaged in the linear and materialistic world, resulting in conflicts, pain and loss of peace and joy.

Most of us are blessed with lots of fortunes and opportunities in life. It would be foolish and arrogant to think that these fortunes and amenities are achieved with our own capabilities. Many people are more competent than us who are not as fortunate as we are to have all these opportunities and fortunes; it underlies the need for our moral responsibility, love and compassion towards the less fortunate people. Are we doing justice to ourselves and others? We need a deep introspection.

Neuroscientists tell us that children's brains are naturally structured to be happy. Look at the life of children—they are happy, healthy, playful, peaceful, energetic and loving all the time, unless there are some compelling reasons to feel and behave otherwise. Nature also envisages that human beings evolve spiritually and lead an awakened life. This is evident from the fact that the brainstem, which regulates survival functions of the body, matures early in life, followed by the limbic or emotional brain, which is associated with learning, memory, emotional experiences, reactions, logical thinking, self-images, etc. The neocortex and prefrontal cortex (PFC) develop and mature during the latter part of a person's 20s; these areas of the brain are associated with the rational approach in life, connectedness with others, higher awareness, various spiritual experiences, etc. It shows that nature envisages human beings to evolve spiritually and have a spiritually awakened life over a period of time.

What Happens When We Are in the Negative Zone?

When we grow up, we complicate life by being stuck at the level of the ego-mind, identifying with the emotional mind and false images, and manifesting the perceptions and beliefs of the subconscious mind. When most of our thoughts and emotions are negative and recur daily, corresponding brain circuits are strengthened and a negative pattern is developed. This way, the ego-mind or subconscious mind ensures that we are always in the same negative zone. Our negative thoughts generate negative emotions, such as fear, anger, hostility, aggression, hatred, frustration, jealousy, insecurity, shame, guilt, depression, sadness, helplessness, anxiety, worry, tension, nervousness as well as corresponding behavioural patterns.

A lifestyle characterized by stress, conflict and pain is a natural outcome staying in the negative zone. A stressful lifestyle has far-reaching consequences. Of course, we need to turn on the stress response in certain unfavourable situations and prepare our bodies and minds to face the threat, which is a natural phenomenon. The problem becomes critical when we get stuck with the stress response for a long time, even after the situation is over, or create a stress response by remembering past stressful situations or anticipating unfavorable life circumstances in the future. These types of responses are the handiwork of the ego-mind for creating stress, conflict and pain to feed on and strengthen the ego-mind itself. When it is severe, frequent and prolonged, it wreaks havoc in our body and mind, creating many adverse consequences. As the ego-mind justifies it, we cannot turn off such stress responses in the absence of higher awareness and switch over to a positive zone.

Studies at the Ohio State University College of Medicine have shown that conflict, pain and stress depress the healing processes in the body and are the main reasons for most illnesses.[5] Negative emotions are found to be significantly correlated with higher death rates from cardiovascular diseases, cancer and myocardial infarction. It is reported that most cases of cancers are linked to the level of stress people experience. The spread of cancer cells requires cooperation amongst them, and this process is accelerated by stress. Ming Wu, José Carlos Pastor-Pareja and Tian Xu report that the stress hormone, adrenaline, produced for a longer period triggers the spread of ovarian cancer cells.[6] It also activates an enzyme called focal adhesion kinase or FAK that inhibits or prevents the destruction of cancer cells.[7] The enzyme that prevents prostate cancer cells is also destroyed by adrenaline.[8]

It is also reported that high level of stress over a long time upregulates the expression of cancer genes in our bodies. Stress hormones, such as cortisol, at higher levels damage mitochondria, the energy storage for cells, which causes fatigue and exhaustion. The Ohio State University Medical Centre found in a study that 170 genes are affected by stress, and out of those, 100 get deactivated completely, which are associated with producing proteins to facilitate healing in the body.[9]

A study of Medical College of Georgia, which spread over a span of 25 years, found that those who have a hostile attitude are five times more prone to getting coronary heart diseases.[10] When we are constantly in the negative zone and stressed, many cells die early, necessitating more cell divisions, which fasten the aging process. In addition to health, the negative zone adversely affects all aspects of our lives. It causes conflicts, spoils relationships, cordiality, peace of mind, happiness, joy and all the enjoyments and thrills in life. Due to the absence of higher awareness and wisdom, we create a life burdened with unhappiness, problems, conflicts, stress, emotional pain and ill health, all of which can make our life hellish!

What Happens When We Stay in the Positive Zone?

A human being is a unique creature in the universe; all the wisdom and richness of the world and the universe are at his command. The creator has provided innumerable and unlimited opportunities with microscopic precision to help us have a fulfilling and 'flowering' life.

When we are in a positive zone with a rational approach to a life based on positive thoughts and emotions, like love and compassion, our brain and mind will have new experiences. Humour and laughter have a great impact on health. The impact of positive emotions on health has been highlighted in many studies.[11] A study by the University of Zurich found that genuine generosity and compassion will cause positive changes in the neural patterns and brain changes, and promote happiness.[12] Neurotransmitters are created in the brain, mainly depending on the nature of the emotions we experience. For example, when we experience love and compassion, it produces serotonin, dopamine, endorphins, oxytocin and anandamide. (Western medical science recently accepted the Sanskrit term *'ananda'*, meaning bliss).[13] Serotonin is associated with mental satisfaction and an elevated state of mind, and it helps one experience a state of peace and serenity. Dopamine is associated with the sensation of reward or pleasure, and it depresses many tendencies for serious illness. Endorphins block the experience of pain and promote happiness. They also help a person experience a sense of detachment from the body and reduce the rigidity of the self-centered ego-mind. Oxytocin is known as the bonding hormone, creating a bond between people, and stimulates a sense of closeness and intimacy with others. It also helps to move beyond the body consciousness, experience the non-local mind or consciousness and broaden our perception beyond that of the ego-mind. It is said that after childbirth, mothers have a high amount of oxytocin in the body, as bonding with the infant is a natural requirement. Positive emotions, like love and compassion, release oxytocin that shuts off the receptors in amygdala.[14]

When we change our patterns of thought, emotions and lifestyle from the negative zone to the positive zone based on higher awareness, changes in perceptions and beliefs and the practice of mediation, the signals sent from the mind to the body will be in a most receptive low wavelength, triggering cells to heal and grow. After detailed research, Hans J.H. Geesink and Dirk K.F. Meijer reported that the healing of many illnesses and the promotion of health and wellness are possible with the help of certain frequencies of the coherent mind.[15] The effects included healthy gene expressions, higher growth hormone levels, slow aging, better circulation of stem cells, a boost in immunity and reduction of inflammation. The function of growth hormones is to repair and regenerate our cells. Researchers have concluded that lowering stress and adopting a positive lifestyle results in adding about 10 years to a healthy lifespan.[16]

Mayo Clinic conducted a detailed study involving 447 people for a period of 30 years and found that people with a positive frame of mind, the optimists, remain mentally and physically healthier.[17] Duke University studied 866 heart patients and reported that patients who had positive emotions had a 20 per cent more chance of recovery and 11 years longer lifespan.[18]

It is reported that when we reduce stress levels and have

positive thoughts, emotions and lifestyles, we bring about healthy changes in the body.

Per-Henrik Zahl, Jan Maehlen and H. Gilbert Welch found in a study that one-fifth of breast cancer cases are healed by a positive mind and body without medical intervention.[19] Brendan O'Regan and Carlyle Hirshberg said that more than 3,000 cases of cancers have been healed with the power of the mind, positive intentions and lifestyle.[20]

It is found that a positive mind and mirthful laughter produce neuroendocrine and reduce stress hormones.[21] Studies found that positive emotions help in speedy recovery for those suffering from cardiovascular issues caused as a result of constant negative emotions.[22] Another study conducted by the American Heart Association in 2007 showed that a positive outlook and emotion give protection to those who have a family history of heart diseases.[23] It is reported that when a person is in a positive state of mind experiencing emotions like love, bliss, or deep meditation, healthy neurotransmitters like anandamide are produced in large quantities.

So, is it not a medical emergency to transform from the negative zone to the positive zone and to have a fulfilling, transformed and awakened life?

Meditation Does Wonders

It is reported that meditation can trigger the expression of genes that identify and eliminate cancer cells and suppress the growth of tumors. Researchers at the Benson–Henry Institute for Mind-Body Medicine at Massachusetts General Hospital in Boston conducted a detailed study in 2008 in which it was shown that when the participants practised mediation after proper training, it was found that it positively influenced 1,561 genes.[24] Of these,

874 genes were upregulated, improving health, and 687 genes were down-regulated, which were related to the stress responses. Further, it showed that it reduced blood pressure, heart and respiration rate. After referring to many studies, Dr Dawson Church, author of *Mind to Matter*, says, 'Many studies show that meditation has a tremendous positive impact in the brain, whole body and mind, and effect healthy changes that help people to reduce the grip of dense ego-mind, experience higher awareness, and healthy emotions, create new experiences in the brain, and mind facilitating new brain circuits.'[25] Meditators are reported to have higher volumes of brain tissues, better sleep, fewer diseases, increased immunity, enhanced emotional health, reduced inflammation, slower aging, increased intercellular communication, balanced neurotransmitters, greater longevity and less stress. Anandamide produced during meditation reportedly inhibits cancer cells. Meditation is the most effective tool for facilitating transformation towards a positive zone.

Mind Engineering Approach to Transformation and Awakening

So, let us start the mind engineering journey for the transformation towards the positive zone or the destination and awakening. The basic principles of this journey include higher awareness, complete attention to the present and profound experience of the present.

I believe this is the most effective approach for effecting position changes at the root level and transformation. So, let us start with the higher awareness of the basic wisdom required, i.e., the basic questions of our lives. While having higher awareness step by step, our perceptions about everything will gradually change at the subconscious mind level, along with our patterns of thoughts, emotions and behaviour. This higher awareness will help us break free from the control of the ego-mind and anchor our lives in the present moment with deeper experiences. Awareness about the basic questions and goals of life, along with its answers, will enable us to have higher experiences that will change the brain circuits and biochemistry in a healthy way, leading to transformation and awakening.

3

BASIC QUESTIONS AND THE GOAL OF LIFE

We need to start with a higher awareness of our basic questions of life: 'What is the goal of our life?' and 'Who am I?' Higher awareness about these vital questions of life is critical in our journey towards awakening. A deep and higher awareness of the answers to these questions at the experiential level leads us to a state of awakening.

What Is the Primary Goal of Life?

So, what is the goal of life? If you ask 'what is the goal of life?' in a group, there will be many answers—earning more money, getting a job, creating a good image among others, seeking happiness, peace, etc. So, the majority of the answers to the question will be 'happiness' or 'peace'. If we ask again, 'Are you fully happy?' or 'Why are you not happy?', people will say, 'I don't have enough money, a good job' or 'I will be happy after marriage or children's wedding,' and the conditions go on. If you analyse the state of mind of rich and powerful people, you will realize that most of them have more problems, stress, conflict, pain, and less peace and happiness than ordinary people. Daniel Kahneman and Angus Deaton reported that 'High income improves evaluation of life but not emotional well-being.'[1] If we introspect again, we realize that when one condition is fulfilled, another one arises as a chain reaction, and there is no point of time in life when we feel we have fulfilled our wishes and remain happy.

This means that our idea of happiness is a mirage, and when we approach one point, another one arises at a distance. The projected happiness is never a reality; this is because the future is never experienced as a reality. It gives us the awareness that happiness is not derived from fulfilling certain conditions or by achieving or acquiring some material possessions; it is a state of mind arising from within.

Then, the question arises: if it is not based on the outside world and is within, why are we not happy? Why are we unhappy most of the time? If it is a state of mind within us, why can't we decide to be happy? What prevents us from being happy always? These are relevant and big questions. One purpose of the book is to find their answers. One reason why we are not happy is that we get entangled in the illusion of the past and the present. We attribute the reasons for unhappiness to some unpleasant or unfavorable life situations from the past or some anticipated problem in the future. Here, a relevant question arises: when can we be happy in life? Can we be happy in the past or future? Can we live in the past or future? No. When do we live? Only in the present moment, but we perceive that happiness will come in the future. Can we live in the future? Those who have not contemplated on this higher awareness may say 'yes'. Think about it closely. Can we live in the past or future? Show me how do you live tomorrow at 10 a.m. or one hour later. You cannot live tomorrow or even one moment ahead. When tomorrow 10 a.m. comes as the reality, it is in the present moment. So, you cannot live in the past or future; you can live only in the present moment. So when can you be happy? Only in the present moment.[2] Spiritual philosopher Myrko Thum says,

> The present moment is the only thing where there is no time. It is the point between past and future. It is always there, and it is the only point we can access in time. Everything that happens, happens in the present moment... Everything that ever happened and will ever happen can only happen in the present moment. It is impossible for anything to exist outside of it.[3]

This awareness is of a high order. We will address it in detail in subsequent chapters.

Another aspect of happiness or reason for being unhappy is our state of mind—the way we think, feel and behave. If it is within us and within our control, why can't we control our thoughts and emotions to be only positive? Yes, many find this question a little confusing. If we analyse and introspect, we conclude that we are not aware of most of our thoughts, their nature and patterns, and we do not have control over them and their consequent emotions. The answer is still not clear, and another pertinent question arises: if we do not control our thoughts and emotions, then who controls them? Finding answers to these questions is a state of higher awareness and is essential to be clear about our goals in life. So, in the subsequent chapters, we will be addressing these questions and answers in detail.

Happiness is the generic term being used in common parlance; in the spiritual context, the term 'joy' is used to express our innate joy experienced unconditionally from within. C.S. Lewis explained a clear distinction between joy, pleasure and happiness. 'I call it Joy, which is here a technical term and must be sharply distinguished both from Happiness and Pleasure[...]

I doubt whether anyone who has tasted it would ever, if both were in his power, exchange it for all the pleasures in the world'.[4] Gautama Buddha had said, 'When the mind is pure, joy follows like a shadow that never leaves.' Why can't we have a joyous state of mind? We have seen that real happiness or joy is to be found within, which means it is a state of mind.[5] The state of mind means the way we think and feel. Then the question seems easy: why can't we have only positive thoughts and feelings? Are we able to regulate our thoughts and feelings always or at any point in time? No. If joy or its absence is the result of our own thoughts and feelings, why can't we avoid negative thoughts and emotions and have only positive thoughts that always create joy? Contemplate.

Are we not able to control and regulate our own thoughts and emotions? The fact that we are unhappy most of the time proves that we are not able to control our own thoughts and emotions. Deliberately, no sane person will choose unhappiness; if we are not able to control our own thoughts and emotions, who is controlling them? This a big question, we need to find the answer. It is essential to find answers to these questions; rather, it should be our goal in life. For the time being, let us be clear that we have no control over most of our thoughts, emotions and behaviours, and treat it as the reason for our unhappiness. We will go into its details and find out the answers later.

Another relevant question now is: if not me, who is controlling my thoughts and emotions, who is this controller? Who am I? Let us see.

4

WHO AM I?

This is the simplest question, and at the same time, the most difficult one humanity has ever addressed. 'Who are you?' is the simplest and the first question we address when interacting with strangers. We answer this question by telling our name, role or other identity, depending on the situation.

If somebody is asking you where you are, you will raise your hand or point to yourself, indicating that 'I am here'. It means that physically 'I am here', and you refer to your body for your individual identity. It means you are body conscious, and at that point of time, you identify with the body. 'I' means my body. If asked again, 'Do you mean you are only body and nothing else? Does a person mean only body?' You will answer, 'Person means body and mind.'

Usually, we refer to the non-physical entity, which is driving us, with a common term called mind. We know that we are driven or controlled by our minds in common parlance, including our thoughts and emotions.

If we ask 'Do we mean a person means only body and mind or anything else?' We may then get a little confused.

Now let us see it minutely.

We have seen that people often identify with physique and body identity. If a bodybuilder says, 'I am strong', he refers to his body. But if an executive says, 'I am under severe stress,' he refers to his emotional mind.

Here we are clear that a person has primarily two aspects, body as well as mind.

Now let us understand this more closely. Suppose another executive says to his spouse, 'Today my mind is disturbed, let us go out for dinner.' Here, one more entity emerges, the other 'I', which is capable of observing and being aware of the disturbed mind and deciding to go out for dinner. Who is this entity or 'I'? Who is this awareness? This awareness is the real essence of you, your true self or consciousness, or the real you! But we need to become aware of it in depth.

Now, let us address the big question, 'Who am I?' in more detail, as its awareness at the experiential level itself is the state of awakening.

We know that a young child is only body-conscious. When we grow up, we identify with our names, forms, roles and images, like 'I am a businessman', 'I am a member of X group with certain ideology'; we may feel that we are respected people in society. Here, we identify with our image, which means we are predominantly image or role conscious. Our predominant identity has shifted from the body to a mind-created image. We have seen that many people are even prepared to die for the ideology they believe in or the roles they play. We have seen people saying, 'I am angry', 'I am disturbed', etc., which means they identify with an emotional mind.

We have seen that there are two non-physical entities: the mind-created image or ego-mind and the true self or consciousness. We are usually fully identified with our image created by the ego-mind which includes our roles, wishes and perceptions. So when we refer to ourselves, we refer to that image without being aware of our true self.

As the ego-mind is an entity in itself, it will not allow us, in the normal course, to have any other awareness or identity that is against its belief. This has been the challenge of all spiritual wisdom and traditions of humanity—to make people aware of who they really are. So, various spiritual gurus used many examples and metaphors to explain and make us believe the reality or truth. It is like a person 'possessed' with an evil spirit. We have seen in movies that a person fully possessed by an evil spirit is not aware of it, and he believes he is what the evil spirit thinks, feels and directs him to behave. He identifies with the evil spirit. As awareness about identification with ego-mind image is a turning point in life and the spiritual journey, we need to be aware of it at a deeper level, but the ego-mind resists such awareness. Let us understand this with the help of an example.

A powerful king, X, had a teenage son, and king of the rival nation, Y, wanted to attack X but could not because X was much stronger than Y. So, Y made an evil plan to harm the prince of X by sending an evil spirit to him by performing witchcraft. The evil spirit started working by creating negative thoughts, emotions, behaviour, conflicts and pain in the prince's mind. The prince fully identified with the evil spirit. His health started deteriorating and he started creating a lot of problems for himself and others. King X got worried and finally engaged a spiritual guru to find the solution. The spiritual guru became aware of the reality and told the facts to King X.

The guru was given the task of saving the prince. He started telling the prince about what had happened to him and the consequences it could bring over a period of time. Initially, he resisted becoming aware of any image of him other than what was created by the evil spirit. Whatever was told by the guru was being misinterpreted by the evil spirit to the prince, so that the words of the guru could not influence him. The guru understood this, and reduced the influence of the evil spirit on the prince by using some special methods to weaken it. As the strength of the evil spirit weakened gradually, the prince started reflecting on the wisdom and became aware of it. He started becoming aware of the evil spirit. This gave him confidence and he decided to come out of the influence of the evil spirit. The moment he became aware of the existence and influence of the evil spirit on him, the latter started losing its strength and control. Gradually, the spiritual guru made him aware of all the wrong perceptions, beliefs and lifestyle created by the evil spirit. This had been denying him the life of an all-powerful prince. The higher awareness and wisdom set him free from the control of the evil spirit entirely and helped him lead the life of a prince.

This is the position each one of us are in. We are not aware that now we are fully identified with the ego-mind. The ego-mind will resist even the slightest attempt to tell us that we are under its control as it is the one doing the interpretations for us. The fact is that you are stronger and more powerful than the image created by the ego-mind, and what you think and feel. We are part of the all-powerful almighty. Why all the spiritual gurus and wisdom had failed to make us believe this truth has been explained in a later chapter. The task of this book is to make us aware of the fact that we are not the evil spirit (ego-mind), and to make us aware of our true self, who we are and help us lead a happy and fulfilling life.

Now, the big question is why we cannot become aware of this truth or realize this wisdom at the experiential level. When this truth is available as awareness and experience, only then it makes sense. All spiritual traditions, right from the Vedas, realized this truth that human being is consciousness or spiritual being, but mostly failed to pass on this wisdom to humanity at the experiential level. Let us try to understand the reason. Becoming aware of the reason itself is awareness of a higher order in the journey towards transformation or awakening.

In order to help us find answer to the question 'who am I?' I would like to share a story told by Swami Vivekananda. A lion cub happened to live along with a group of sheep. Since the cub lived and grew up along with sheep, it developed their lifestyle and nature, despite growing up as a lion physically. One day, another lion came to the jungle and found a group of sheep and a lion living together. The lion was surprised to see that and felt offended seeing another lion living like sheep.

The visitor lion wanted to convince the other lion and said, 'You are not a sheep, but a lion like me, the all-powerful king of the jungle.'

The other lion was not convinced and said, 'No, I am a sheep, like the other sheep, and I am okay with it.'

The visiting lion did not give up. He took the other one to a nearby lake and showed him his reflection, and said, 'You see your shape, you are like me, you roar.'

The lion got convinced that he was not a sheep; he roared and started hunting other animals, and lived as the king of the jungle.

We are in the same position—we are not what we think we are. We are much more unique and powerful, and we deserve a better fulfilling life. We need to bring in a shift in awareness about who we are, at the experiential level, which is the purpose of the book and the mind engineering process. As there is a strong tendency to continue with the same beliefs and perceptions, and there is strong resistance from the ego-mind, we need deeper awareness about this wisdom or truth.

With these brief introductory deliberations on the question 'who am I?' let us take a deep dive into it. This 'deep dive' is like a diver trying to find a precious ruby from the bottom of the sea. For us, the most precious gift in life is the answer to this question at the experiential level. As this is a very basic and subtle level of wisdom, we need to approach it in detail to become clearly aware of it.

Once the answer to this question is received at the experiential level as wisdom, it becomes the state of spiritual awakening and the end of all problems and sufferings in life. So this is the most critical level of awareness in the process of awakening. All spiritual traditions, including the Vedas, consisting the ancient spiritual wisdom of India, which are believed to have been written between 1500 and 1200 BC, also addressed this question during the transition period from Bronze Age to Iron Age.

Why is this the toughest question of humanity? We have seen the resistance of the ego-mind. Nobody can understand 'who am I' intellectually. We cannot think and understand the answer with our mind, which we are identified with; we can find the answer only as awareness and experience. When we become fully aware of the ego-mind's patterns and do not identify with them, the blockades will be removed, the awareness of who we are, the consciousness, will automatically emerge. To put in an example, if we remove the sunglass, the brightness will automatically emerge. The mind engineering wisdom will help us remove the blockades or deactivate them. One way to facilitate the removal of the blockades and move closer to the realization that we are 'consciousness' is to bring in more awareness about it. The experience of the present moment, the practice of nurturing positive thoughts and emotions, like love and compassion, and the practice of meditation will prepare our brain and mind to realize this higher wisdom. Human beings have an ability to believe and visualize, and the visualized experience is as good as experiencing reality. The brain or mind does not distinguish between what is real and what is visualization if it is done with complete belief. Such experiences will make corresponding changes in the brain, weakening the brain circuits supporting the ego-mind and will help us have a deeper realization and experience of 'who we are,' the consciousness. The answer to this question at the experiential level is the ultimate wisdom one can have, and, therefore, answer to this question is the most important in life. So, the transformation or awakening means a shift from the body and ego-mind identity to a higher awareness at the experiential level that we are pure consciousness or spiritual beings with human experiences.

We receive and become aware of all the knowledge from the material world through sensory perceptions, but this wisdom, answer to the question 'who am I' cannot be understood, accessed and experienced through sensory signals or with an analytical mind. In the normal course, we do not become aware of this reality through sensory signals because the ego-mind interprets all sensory signals as per its nature of perceptions, beliefs and images. If we become aware of the wisdom that we are consciousness, the ego-mind loses its control, its existence comes under threat, and we no longer identify with it. So, the ego-mind resists or misinterprets any new wisdom or experience, as it threatens the present position, existence and survival of the ego-mind itself. This wisdom of consciousness is the death knell for the ego-mind. So, normally it will not allow us to have this wisdom at any cost. Great spiritual gurus were aware of this fact, so most of the ancient spiritual teachings on consciousness were indirect communicated through similes, stories or metaphors with a view to bypass the resistance and interpretation of the ego-mind and register the ideas or wisdom deep into the subconscious mind.

So, one of the earliest Upanishads, Kena Upanishad,

addresses this most difficult question, 'Who are you?' and explains consciousness indirectly through a question-answer series between a student and teacher.

As part of the question, the student said, 'I am aware that this is the essence of my life, I am aware that the outside world is experienced in the inside world, I am aware that physical matter cannot produce these subjective experiences, I am aware that one energy force is shining through me.' The student asked, 'What is that illumines my vision or other senses, which subtle energy or light enables me to experience the sensory perceptions or the subjective experiences of the five senses.'

The teacher tried to answer the question, initially addressing it in a general way, saying that the question and the answer are most important for humanity, which is the greatest secret of human life. Then the teacher attempted to answer it directly and said, 'It is the eye of the eye, it is the ear of the ear…it is the mind of the mind.' The teacher indicated that all sensory perceptions and experiences, including the subjective experiences in mind, happen within this energy field or consciousness, and this energy field is an energy body or etheric body that regulates and manifests through the physical body, sensory experiences and functions. It implies that this is not part of the body, but the body exists within this force. It pervades all parts of the body.

As the student was not convinced about the indirect answer, he asked, 'How do I know about it realistically?'

The teacher expressed his inability, and said, 'I do not know how to express it because senses cannot perceive, and neither mind nor any language can explain it, and you cannot think about it and understand.' As the student was not satisfied, the teacher explained further, saying that his guru had explained it to him this way: 'It is not something that is known, it is unknown; at the same time, it is not unknown.' The answer was like a riddle, again not direct. The inference can be drawn that the guru was indicating the answer that, in fact, consciousness is 'you, yourself', and that is the real essence of you.

In Chandogya Upanishad, there is a story of a father trying to teach his son what is supreme self or consciousness. Through many examples, he explains the 'force' within which everything exists, which permeates everything, which is the source of everything. Finally, he says you are that *'thatwamasi'*—there is no difference between you and the supreme self or Almighty, you are part of it.

The role of this book or a real spiritual teacher is like that of the visitor lion, to convince people that we are not what we are thinking about ourselves (the ego-mind), but we are much more precious, powerful and unique spiritual beings deserving much higher awareness and better quality of life.

It is easier said than becoming aware of it. We have a long way to go before we become aware of this information as wisdom at the experiential level. Let us have a deeper awareness of it from the mind engineering model and let us start understanding mind and consciousness at a deeper level.

5

MIND ENGINEERING MODEL OF MIND AND CONSCIOUSNESS

In common parlance, mind refers to the non-physical aspect of a human being. All disciplines and schools of thought tell us that there are different parts of the mind. It is essential to have in-depth awareness about this truth, which is necessary to be free from the control of the ego-mind and continue our journey towards awakening. So, let us take a closer look at it for clear and deep awareness.

We need to understand the basic dynamics of the mind and consciousness. Different people or schools of thought understand and describe the mind differently; the operational definitions of the mind and its parts are different for different authors. The terms subconscious mind, consciousness, mind and ego-mind are used interchangeably by different authors. So, for the sake of clear understanding, let us take a closer look at the basic concepts as referred to by the vast majority of authors on the subject. This will give us clear and higher awareness about ourselves and others and answers to the basic questions about who we are at a deeper level. We have become aware of the broad classification of the mind or fundamental truth taught by all spiritual traditions and different disciplines that there are two non-physical entities within a person.

Two Non-Physical Entities

The existence of two non-physical entities with distinct qualities and nature has been substantiated by the studies by Dr Andrew Newberg and the late Dr Eugene G. d'Aquili in their famous book *Why God Won't Go Away: Brain Science and the Biology of Belief*.[1] Experiences of peace, tranquility and bliss are results of the awakened state of consciousness, which is associated with the right hemisphere of the brain. Since the left brain consists of more number of neurons, synaptic connections and wirings, which processes thoughts, emotional patterns and experiences of the subconscious mind, the left brain dominates and inhibits the right brain. Still, the true self is the source of higher awareness, love, peace, joy and higher emotions of compassion which are processed by the right brain and neocortex area. By now, we have clear awareness that we are living consciousness, and we also have awareness and experience of what is the ultimate wisdom we can achieve—that in itself is the awakening.

Right from the Vedas to modern-day body-mind science, we have been told that there are mainly two parts of the mind. Mandukya Upanishad (Verse 3.1.1) conveys this truth through an example of a tree (body) and two birds on it; one eats the fruit and has various experiences, and the other one observes it—that is the conscious presence. It implies that the feeding bird is the ego-mind which has various sensory experiences, and the other is conscious awareness of everything. Different schools of behavioural science also advocate distinct parts of the mind. Though there are different schools of thought and different terminologies used to describe it, the most widely accepted terminologies to identify these two parts are:

i. Ego-mind, and
ii. True self

Ego-Mind

The ego-mind is the emotional mind or the self-image of ourselves. We all have an overall image of ourselves. The ego-mind's basic approach is emotional, either relating to the past or future. Its fundamental nature is to have conflicts, mental pain, a basic sense of fear, a sense of separateness and a sense of lack in different degrees in life. It always drives thoughts, feelings and behaviour corresponding to our image, perceptions and beliefs. It always perceives the past and future as realities and reacts to them emotionally. The ego-mind is always in conflict, relating to the past or future, and its attention is not in the present moment or now. This ego-mind is our driving force almost all the time, and hence we are not able to think, feel and behave rationally and independently with 'free-will'. It has two parts: the conscious mind (not consciousness, which we address later) and the subconscious mind.

Conscious mind

It refers to the part of our emotional mind or images that we are aware of. It is the creative mind that can think, aspire, feel and do things differently in different situations. We have many roles and corresponding images in society and our family, and we consciously identify with these roles and images. We believe that 'I' means the totality of these roles, images, related thoughts, feelings, behaviours and desires. We are or can become conscious/aware of it. The conscious mind wants to fulfil a lot of its unlimited desires, like happiness, mental peace, health, wealth, positions, good relationships, etc., through these roles, but the fact is that we never really fulfil these desires completely at any point of time, and the end result is the opposite—we never feel fulfilled, completely happy, contended, healthy, peaceful and stress-free. Though many people have achieved a lot in life in terms of comfort, good health, wealth, position, etc., the end result is always the same. Most of the time, they are in some sort of pain, fear, conflict, sufferings, stress or sense of lack, never fully content or happy. We spend a lot of time, energy and money to achieve the above desires or goals of our conscious mind, but we fail miserably. Some sort of mental pain is the basic nature and part of our lives, and as everybody experiences it in differing degrees always, this mind pattern is taken as natural or common. But this part of the mind that we think we are aware of is only a small part of us, and that is why we cannot control the negative patterns of thought, emotions or behaviours, even if we want to be free of them. For example, a person who gets angry frequently is aware of his behaviour, but he cannot control or change this behaviour despite his best efforts because the major part of our mind is the subconscious mind.

Subconscious mind

Subconscious mind refers to that part of the ego-mind of which we are not aware. Different authors have used different terminologies to refer to this part of the mind. Sigmund Freud initially used the term 'subconscious', and later used the term 'unconscious' instead of 'subconscious'. In the normal course, we are not aware of how it originates, operates, generates thoughts and emotions, drives our behavioural patterns and manifests. Deep awareness about the subconscious mind will answer many of our questions, like, why each person thinks, feels and behaves differently, why we cannot control our negative thoughts, emotions, behavioural patterns, who we are, etc. Scientists estimate that the subconscious mind drives about 95 per cent of our thoughts, feelings and behaviours. Ninety-five per cent of who you are by the time you are 35 years old relies on a set of memorized behaviours, skills, emotional reactions, beliefs, perceptions and attitudes that function like a subconscious automatic computer programme.[2]

The subconscious mind is the foundation of our personality. It includes our belief system, basic self-image and perception of self, others and different life situations. Up to the age of about seven, brains of the children are in a theta wave pattern and perceive experiences without analytical capacity; all experiences are recorded as felt or experienced along with attended emotions without being aware of the intentions or rationale behind various experiences or happenings.[3] For example, a child being scolded by parents may believe that something is wrong with him and may think, 'I am inferior to others, that is why I am scolded.' He is not able to analytically understand the good intentions of his parents. By the age of seven, children experience different emotions from various experiences, draw conclusions, develop a belief system and pattern of perception, and form self-image based on these experiences, which become the basis of their personalities. These experiences of emotions are deposited, like energy storage, in the mind and become the foundation of the ego-mind and personality. The experiences thereafter, which have similar resonance, add up to earlier deposits of experiences and emotions and strengthen it. With the same example, we can say that a child, who is scolded even after he is seven years old, or one who has undergone similar experiences will have the same emotional experience and add it to the earlier emotional storage. Brain circuits are developed corresponding to these experiences and provide the supporting system to the subconscious mind. As it is the major portion of our mind, it becomes the dominant driving force of our patterns of thoughts, emotions and behaviours in life. It operates like a default computer programme that functions automatically and drives us as programmed. This is why it is not practically possible to control or change the thoughts, emotions and behavioural patterns as per the desires of our conscious mind.

Internal conflict

Subtle conflicts are always taking place within us, and that is the one reason behind the absence of peace and happiness in life, thus resulting in mental and physical health problems. Conflict is between the subconscious mind and the conscious mind. The basic image of the subconscious mind and that of the conscious mind may be of opposite nature. The subconscious mind is substantially very strong, and as Tor Nørretranders puts it, while the subconscious mind is like an autopilot, the conscious mind is the conscious driver. The subconscious mind processes some two crore stimuli per second, while the conscious mind process 40 environmental stimuli per second.[4] This creates an internal conflict within us with a lot of consequences.

Let us see one more example. In her childhood, a girl was (believed to have had) hurt, neglected and had belittling experiences. She had corresponding emotions deposited in the subconscious mind and had conclusions like, 'I am inferior to others', 'I am not up to the mark', etc. This led to the development of behavioural traits like isolation, fear of public speaking and introversion. But being an intelligent girl, suppose she becomes an executive—it would require her to interact frequently with groups and address gatherings. She may experience a lot of stress and face difficulty in group interactions, especially while addressing gatherings. She would want to avoid interactions with others, but the conscious mind would still want to be able to have stress-free interactions with others. It does not mean that all who have had a similar experience in childhood would have the same personality traits when they grew up.

Another girl with a similar experience may seek more attention and appreciation of others and like interactions with others. No two people have identical experiences and conclusions from the same situations. The extent of the internal conflict between the conscious and subconscious mind is different for all of us. This remains an area of great concern and a source of stress for all of us; this is why we cannot think, feel and behave the way our conscious mind wants and have an image and life as per its desire.

Let us take the example of a police officer, whose conscious mind wants others to perceive him as daring and brave. However, due to childhood experiences of threat, he has deep-rooted fear in his subconscious mind, and he fails miserably in being able to put forth an image of a bold police officer. The fact that we are not aware of is that the subconscious mind and its image are much stronger than the conscious mind. In the police officer's case, the subconscious mind manifests its image by way of his tone, sound, body language, behavioural patterns, personality traits, the activity of mirror hormones, etc., as a fearful man, and overshadows the brave image the conscious mind wants to manifest. Keeping in mind both these examples, we can introspect and become aware of the internal conflict within us. When our conscious mind has needs and images that may be contradictory to our subconscious mind, we are practically resisting the subconscious mind perceptions and beliefs unsuccessfully unless the reprogramming is done. Subconscious mind will devise its strategies to assert its superiority and prevail over the conscious mind. It is said that 'what is resisted persists'. As part of reprogramming, an exercise of close observation of our videos of different situations will reveal these manifestations of the subconscious mind, and we can bring in more awareness, which can help us change the subconscious mind patterns.

True Self or Consciousness

The true self is the true essence of a person, the non-physical entity, the 'beingness' of humans. It is the essence or spirit, or divine element of human beings. We have found that there are two non-physical entities of a human being: the ego-mind and consciousness. We are able to think, feel and behave out of 'free will' because of our consciousness. When driven by the true self, we do everything rationally, rather than driven by compulsive patterns of the ego-mind or conscious mind images. This is the real you. The basic nature of the true self is love, peace and joy. This is our basic natural state.

Look at children—they are mostly happy, peaceful and playful. Neuroscientists say that our brains are naturally structured or wired to be happy. It operates from a platform of rationality. When true self drives us, every thought, feeling or action is of a high order and quality. We are rooted in the present, and reference to past or future is made to a limited extent. The experience or quality of life driven by the true self is of the highest order. Many authors refer to the true self as a synonym to consciousness or the divine aspect of human beings. In terms of quantum physics, everything is energy and everything exists in consciousness; the human consciousness is part of the larger cosmic consciousness. The neocortex and right hemisphere of the brain are predominantly associated with the operation of the true self. Basically, our emotions are love, peace and joy, and our approach towards daily activities is rational.

The inference made from the above observation is that by

nature, we are programmed to be happy and healthy unless there are compelling reasons, like loss of something precious, absence of essential things for survival, illness or genuine threat to life, etc. On the other hand, in reality, the vast majority of our thoughts in a day are negative; we react to every situation with negative emotions creating mental pain; we have compelling and addictive patterns of thinking and feeling; our behaviour is such that it creates stress, conflict and pain most of the time. At a deeper level, we are aware that something is wrong somewhere and something precious is missing in life. From this faint awareness of the conscious mind, a deep urge pops up to be happy and peaceful in life. People frequently introspect, though unsuccessfully, and resort to activities, like reading self-help books, doing meditation, yoga, pranayama, exercises, training and wellness programmes, etc., but the ultimate goal is still not achieved. I am not saying that these are not helpful. But unless we become aware of and address the problem at its root level, the expected transformation may not be achieved.

To put the idea in a metaphor, each one of us is like the Earth. When the ego-mind drives us, it generates negative thoughts and emotions, which are like pollution and smoke produced on Earth. The thick smoke will not allow the bright light of the sun (cosmic consciousness) to lighten up our lives in its natural way. When we live in the shadow of smoke (ego-mind), life will be miserable and of poor quality. It is natural to have bright sunlight and enlightened life on Earth. The ego-mind is the dense energy field closely covering the entire body, even at the cellular level, that constantly interacts with every part of the body through a communication and biofeedback loop, which manifests in our body. Like in the case of smoke, the manifestation of the consciousness in the body is blocked or interfered with by the ego-mind.

Basic Nature of Consciousness

We have seen that the basic nature of consciousness is love, peace and joy; when we are driven by consciousness, we operate from a platform of rationality with compassion. As part of its basic nature, consciousness perceives everyone as equal and part of the same large spiritual entity and closely interconnected. It wants a harmonious life of compassion and love with others, just like all the living cells in a body. Interconnectedness among human beings has been studied by many researchers. It has been proved that we are all interconnected in the quantum field. A study established a connection between people at the level of consciousness, irrespective of their distance.[5] The brain of a person, who was sitting inside a protected container, responded to the stimulation of their partners outside the containers. In another study, when one partner was shown an image in a distant place, the other partner immediately developed the same pattern of EEG brain function.[6] The brain stimulus sent by the sender was received by the receiver in the identical area in the brain as that of the sender; the receiver's brain reacted as though he was seeing the same image at the same time.

The rational intentions of a person are of higher order and processed and received in the right frontal lobe area. When a teacher sent energy signals to a student, the student showed an increase in the number of alpha brain waves in his right frontal lobe, which implies that this is the area of the brain where the intentional signals are received.[7] Basic oneness is not only the nature of mystical experience but also one of the revelations of modern science.[8]

This higher awareness will help us change our perception of ourselves and others, lead a harmonious life and undergo spiritual development. Dawson Church writes, 'The tools of our consciousness including our beliefs, progress, thoughts, intentions, and faith—often correlate much more strongly with our health, longevity, and happiness than our genes do.'[9]

True self will be experienced only when we are in the present moment. When our ego-mind drives us, it prevents us from being anchored in the present moment. We have seen that every thought, emotion and action that is not essentially relevant to the present moment is the ego-mind strategy to deny us the present. When we are in the present moment, it threatens the very existence of the ego-mind itself, and so it is always the strategy of the ego-mind to deny us the experience of the present moment. When we are distracted by unwanted thoughts, negative emotions and behaviours relating to the past and future, which is happening almost all the time, the ego-mind succeeds and we lose the game. In impolite words, we can say we are fooled by the ego-mind, meaning that if we have any negative emotion as the reaction, it means we are not in the present moment and not experiencing the now and are driven by the ego-mind. The only solution is to have higher awareness and wisdom of who we are at the deepest and experiential level, i.e., we are not human beings with spiritual experiences, but consciousness or spiritual beings with human experiences, the pure living consciousness. So let us take a deep dive into our real essence—consciousness.

Consciousness: A Deep Dive

Historians have recorded that man has shown glimpses of conscious activities and conscious awareness even during preliterate civilizations. Ancient thinkers wrote that the mind exists in a separate spiritual realm—an idea that Plato systematically presented in the fourth century in his text titled

Phaedo. From the seventeenth century onwards, the idea of 'consciousness' attracted the attention of philosophers and scientists worldwide, and was referred to as a phenomenon related to thoughts and mind. But scientists whose works were limited to the material realm and objective evidence-based studies rejected the idea of consciousness and considered the word itself a taboo.

From the early twentieth century, with the advent of quantum physics, the idea of consciousness gained more attention in the scientific community. The mainstream scientific community considered consciousness as a product of the brain and referred to it in the context of being aware/conscious of or related it to the cognitive ability of a human being. But the vital question remained: how could the physical brain produce subjective experiences and subjective awareness in the mind. In the early nineteenth century, eminent psychologists, such as William James and F.W.H. Myers, described consciousness not as a product of the brain but the spiritual essence or entity of a person as taught by all spiritual traditions in different ways.

Broad Perspectives on Consciousness

Consciousness as a cognitive faculty

This perspective views consciousness as a cognitive ability of a human being of becoming aware of various sensory signals. It implies that the brain produces consciousness, and it continues to exist till the death of a person. However, this perspective does not answer the key question which has not been addressed so far. How can the brain cells and neurons, which are physical parts of the body, create a subjective experience, which is the 'hard problem of consciousness'? This is the materialistic or 'reductionist' view of consciousness. Though this is the view of mainstream materialistic science, William James said, 'Our normal waking consciousness, rational consciousness as we call it, is but one special type of consciousness, whilst all about it, parted from it by the filmiest of screens, there lie potential forms of consciousness entirely different'.[10]

Consciousness as the true spiritual essence

This perspective looks at consciousness as the true spiritual essence or entity of human beings, which is part of the larger cosmic consciousness. The basic premise of this perspective is that consciousness is not the result of neuronal activities in the brain, but it is the non-physical essence of human beings, and is the natural driving force of all body functions of human beings and form a part of the larger cosmic consciousness. The scientists and authors who hold this perspective can be referred to as 'spiritual scientists'.

Reductionist Perspective

The reductionist or materialistic approach of science for understanding human beings was greatly influenced by the philosophy of René Descartes, a very influential French philosopher of the seventeenth century and Sir Isaac Newton. Descartes, under the influence of the Church, made a 'Cartesian split' and said that we are concerned with body only, leaving the domain of mind and soul to the Church declaring that 'Anything to do with the soul, mind and emotions, I leave to the clergy. I will only claim the realm of the body.'[11] He considered thought to be a basic feature of human existence, saying, 'I think therefore I am.' Newton, 'the father of modern science', also maintained that only physical matter is real and relevant. For a long time, the beliefs and views of these two influential personalities became the foundation of all the scientific branches, including medical science.

The scientists following this perspective try to explain consciousness as the opposite of the state of being 'unconscious', or what is absent during sleep. Descartes clearly proposed a concept of dualism, which states that the conscious mind is a non-material entity distinct from the physical body. He stated that everything in the world functions like a machine and its parts, including the human body, and provided a basis for reductionism. The materialists or reductionist scientists firmly held the view that consciousness is a product of the brain, and it was taboo to even use the word consciousness till the early nineteenth century in science. George Miller, the founding father of cognitive psychology, in his pioneering book *Psychology: The Science of Mental Life*, went to the extent of proposing to ban the c-word.[12] During the 1980s, the idea of consciousness had become the center stage of mainstream neuroscience research. Neurophysiology considers that our subjective experiences are produced by the brain, but could not explain how the physical brain could produce subjective experiences, which is the 'hard problem of consciousness', as David Chalmers stated.[13]

The science of consciousness proposed by materialists indicates that consciousness primarily includes three key aspects:

i. A state of alertness, when we are awake
ii. The faculty of attention, which can focus our mental resources on particular information and
iii. Conscious access—the ability of man to pay selective attention to something and become aware of

In this context, neuroscientist Antonio Damasio defined consciousness as 'the self in the act of knowing.'[14] The basic premise of the reductionist approach is that the mind and consciousness are the products of neuro-physiological activities and processes in the brain, and all conscious experiences of a human being, such as the experiences of five senses, are purely the result of the activity of the brain circuits. When groups of neurons start firing in an organized manner in the respective areas of the brain, it will impact other areas of the cortex, and the sum total of brain activities produces conscious awareness. This was the view of the vast majority of contemporary scientists until the nineteenth century. Steven Pinker was prominent among those who advocated the materialistic view.[15] The reductionist view was very much popular in the field of medical science in the West, and as substantiated in *Newsweek*: 'Modern neuroscience has shown that there is no user (of the brain). The soul is, in fact, the information processing activity of the brain. The new imaging techniques have tied every thought and emotion to neural activity.'[16]

The Perspective of Spiritual Scientists

This perspective states that there is a grand field of energy, information, intelligence and potential in the universe, the cosmic consciousness or energy field (some refer to it as divinity or Almighty) in which everything exists, including the consciousness of each individual. An increasingly large number of scientists came out with the view that consciousness is not a brain product but is the spiritual essence of human beings. Of course, the brain is closely associated or correlated with human experiences but consciousness is not necessarily caused by the brain. Probably, it was first scientifically validated with a large study by Southampton University in the year 2014, which conclusively proved that consciousness is the spiritual essence of a human being that survives death.[17] In the spiritual context, all religious teachings tell us that human beings are spiritual beings, and the spiritual entity is referred to in different terms, such as consciousness, souls or divine element. That spiritual entity is the essence of a person and is immortal—quantum physics has given validation to this perspective.

The reductionist view dominated Western science, and hence great authors who belonged to the spiritual scientists' view, such as F.W.H Myers, were not well recognized in the West. He had published a seminal piece of work,

Human Personality and its Survival of Bodily Death[18] in 1903, which received high praise from his contemporary William James, who is considered the 'father of American psychology'. Myers proposed the existence of 'subliminal consciousness', which is different from the primary consciousness of human beings. Though the reductionists dominated science, especially the domain of human behavioural science, many authors, like Aldous Huxley, complemented the contributions of Myers. The contributions of Myers and James have been appreciated in the recent past by scientists and authors as spiritual science has gained more acceptance amongst the scientific community.

Quantum Physics Perspective on Consciousness

Quantum physics states that everything is energy at the subatomic level, and everything exists, whether it is at the subatomic level or universal level, in consciousness. The basic principle of quantum physics is the existence of cosmic consciousness as a unified energy field of information and unlimited potentialities, and that everything exists within this force, including the individual consciousness of each human being. Quantum physics systematically studied consciousness from the time of Max Planck in the 1900s. It recognizes the primacy of consciousness, i.e., consciousness creates reality. Leading scientists like Rupert Sheldrake[19], Roger Penrose[20] and Amit Goswami[21] have established that feeling, thinking, intuition, creativity, giving meaning to inputs, decisions, etc., are not functions of the brain alone, but these subjective qualities need a non-physical source, i.e., consciousness. To put it in an example, the picture on the TV screen is not produced by the LEDs or the remote control—it needs a source of telecast externally. But it is a fact that a TV set and remote control are associated with the phenomenon of showing movies on the screen. Even if the TV screen is broken, the telecast of the movie does not stop. It remains within the non-physical realm.

The ancient wisdom of many civilizations, especially in the East, states that consciousness is the real essence of a human being and survives death. The connectedness of consciousness of different people has been part of ancient wisdom and also the basic premise of quantum physics. The parapsychologist Dean Radin proved that the mind of a person in a group of like-minded meditators influences others participating in the group.[22] Sheldrake called this force of consciousness a 'morphogenetic field', which is the source or programme that runs the physical functions of a human being at the minute level of cells and genes.[23] Quantum physics also recognizes that the potentialities of consciousness can collapse into physical realities in different situations.

Manifestation of Consciousness

Many authors have described consciousness as the essence or the spiritual entity of a person, in the context of its many physical manifestations. Referring to the instances of healing warts through hypnotic suggestions, the famous biologist, physician and author Lewis Thomas, referred to this as 'one of the great mystifications of science.'[24] 'Hardly enough for the mind to say, simply, get off, eliminate yourselves, without providing something in the way of specifications as to how to go about it [...] A person in charge, kind of super-intelligence is in all of us infinitely smarter, and possessed of technical know-how far beyond our present understanding.'

It has been conclusively established that physical changes, like healing of warts, can happen through hypnotic suggestions. There are many instances in which it has been established that communication occurs between two like-minded people of similar mental resonance. Louisa E. Rhine reported an incident in which a woman suddenly 'doubled over, clutching her chest as if in severe pain' and said, "Something has happened to Nell (daughter); she has been hurt."[25] Two hours later, there was a communication that Nell had died in a car accident from an injury on her chest two hours before. Rhine[26] and Ian Stevenson[27] reviewed many such cases and proved their accuracy.

The premise that the consciousness of different people is interconnected and is part of larger consciousness has been proved by many studies and through many instances.

Consciousness and the Mystical Experience

Mysticism is the common terminology used to refer to the experience of consciousness as a spiritual entity or living in the experience of consciousness or beingness with awareness. Let us study the words of some great scientists and authors on mystical experience.

Henry Price wrote, 'No philosophy of human personality is worth very much unless it takes full account of the data of mystical experience.'[28] C.D. Broad says, 'I think it more likely than not that in religious and mystical experience men come into contact with some reality or some aspect of reality which they do not come into contact with any other way.'[29] William James identified two main characteristics of mystical experiences:

  i. **Ineffability:** Ineffability means the difficulty in expressing or conveying mystical subjective experiences in words or language to others. This has been expressed by many people who had out of body experience (OBE) or near-death experiences (NDE) and could not fully express it in words.

  ii. **Noetic quality:** People who had mystical experiences were found to have gained fundamental insight and profound wisdom on various aspects of life and the universe. James further says that it gives the impression that the source of this wisdom is from a region originating from outside normal consciousness.[30]

Canadian psychiatrist R.M. Bucke termed his own mystical experience as one of 'cosmic consciousness' and spent the latter part of his life further investigating this subject.[31] He describes the mystical experience in his own words as: 'I found myself wrapped in a flame-colored cloud. For an instant, I thought of fire, an immense conflagration somewhere close by in that great city; the next, I knew that the fire was within myself.' He further felt that there came upon a sense of exultation, immense joyousness and intellectual illumination, which was impossible to describe; he realized that there is living presence of consciousness in the whole universe and eternal life, and all men are immortal.

Ancient thinkers like Plato, Spinoza and Heraclitus have

believed and narrated various aspects of mystical experiences. Bertrand Russell has quoted Heraclitus talking about mystical experiences, 'In such a nature we see the true union of the mystic and the man of science that the highest eminence, as I think, that it is possible to achieve in the world of thought.'[32] William James says that overcoming all the barriers between the individual and the Absolute is a great mystic achievement. He writes, 'In mystic states, we both become one with the Absolute, and we become aware of our oneness. This is the everlasting and triumphant mystical tradition, hardly altered by differences of clime or creed. In Hinduism, in Neoplatonism, in Sufism, in Christian mysticism, in Vietnaminism, we find the same recurring note, so that there are about mystic utterances an eternal unanimity which ought to make a critic stop, and think.'[33] Walter Terence Stace identified the following properties of mystical experience:

i. A sense of objectivity
ii. A strong positive effect with calmness, joy, peace, blessedness, etc.
iii. A feeling of something holy, sacred or divine in contact with something powerful
iv. A sense of positive experience which is not as per the ordinary rules of logic, and
v. The ineffability of the experiences, a sense of unity, and oneness cannot be explained in words, which is the common characteristic cited by all the authors.[34]

Meister Eckhart remarked, 'Here all blades of grass, food and stone, all things are one.'[35] As per Stace, 'Undifferentiated unity is the essence of the introvertive mystical experience.'[36]

Referring to consciousness, the Mandukya Upanishad says that beyond ordinary dreaming and dreamless sleep, there lies the higher form, *turia*, i.e., fourth consciousness, which is described as:

> The Fourth, say the wise, is not subjective experience nor objective experience, nor experience intermediate between these two, nor is it a negative condition which is neither consciousness nor unconsciousness. It is not the knowledge of the senses, nor is its relative knowledge, nor yet inferential knowledge. Beyond the senses, beyond the understanding beyond all expressions, is The Fourth. It is pure unitary consciousness, wherein awareness of the world and multiplicity is completely obliterated. It is ineffable peace. It is the supreme good. It is One without a second. It is the Self. Know it alone.[37]

The Sufis use the term '*fana*' to describe a mystical experience, which means passing away. It implies that we must shed our personal identifications or obliterate or transcend our ego-mind to access the higher consciousness.

The mystical experiences of Arthur Koestler received a lot of attention. Koestler reported his own mystical experiences in his imprisonment during the Spanish Civil War in 1937.[38] He was a well-educated and a committed socialist activist. He felt he was floating on his back in a river of peace, under bridges of silence, and it came from nowhere and flowed nowhere, and the 'I' had ceased to exist. He says that it was a concrete experience. In fact, its primary mark was that the sensation was more real than any other he had experienced before and that the veil had fallen, and was in touch with 'real reality', the hidden order of things, the X-ray texture of the world, normally obscured by layers of irrelevancy. He writes, "'I' ceases to exist because it has, by a kind of mental osmosis, established communication with, and been dissolved in the universal pool. It is this process of dissolution and limitless expansion, which is sensed as the "oceanic feeling" as the draining of all tensions, the absolute catharsis, the peace that passeth all understanding.'[39]

There have been many skeptics about mystical experiences of consciousness among material scientists. Neurological explanations were prominent among the sceptics. It was explained that the neurological state called temporal lobe epilepsy (TLE) could result in mystical experiences and a shift in consciousness. Among the skeptics, J.L. Saver and J. Rabbin proposed TLE for mystical experiences.[40] Later, it was found that out of the 15 cases studied, only two had the chance of having TLE seizures and some shift in consciousness. However, Henri Gastaut conducted a detailed study involving thousands of cases by himself and several other clinical epileptologists, but could not find even a single unambiguous case of TLE in mystical experiences.[41] Hubert Thruston conducted a detailed study and substantiated on mystical experiences and the luminous phenomena.[42]

W. Penfield and P. Perot studied 523 TLE patients, and only about 10 per cent had reported some sort of seizure patterns and shift in consciousness, but none of them had any resemblance to mystical experiences of consciousness.[43] Subsequently, studies by E. Halgren, R.D. Walter, D.G. Cherlow, P.H. Crandall and P. Gloor confirmed this pattern.[44] Freud initially did not recognize the mystical experiences, but later, he changed his impression when his own close friend Roland Romain went through it and witnessed the changes personally. Later, Freud acknowledged it and wrote 'a peculiar feeling[…]a sensation of eternity […] as of something limitless, unbounded-as it were oceanic […] a feeling of an indissoluble bond, being one with the eternal world as whole.'[45] Carl Jung had an accepting view of mystical experiences. Erich Neumann describes mystical experiences as 'a fundamental category of human experience [...] the profoundest source of creative life [...] means very center is an unknown creative force which lives within him, and molds him in ever-new forms and transformations.'[46] C.D. Broad reports: 'I think it more likely than not that in religious, and mystical experience men come into contact with some reality or some aspect of reality which they do not come into contact within any other way.'[47] Famous psychologist G. Foster had a mystical experience and reported that it was an overwhelming sense of numinous contact with a loving but invisible being whose presence was keenly felt and sharply localized in space. This 'vision' and experience lasted for five days, and it awakened her and transformed her life.[48] S.D. Kirlian discovered a technology to photograph the human aura in 1939, which attracted the attention of the scientific community.[49] Subsequently, Russian physicist K. Korotkov discovered gas discharge visualization technique to picturize the 'biofield' or bioenergy field of a living organism, which was extensively used for diagnosing health issues.[50] Einstein said, 'Everyone who is seriously involved in the pursuit of science becomes convinced that a spirit is manifest in the laws of the Universe, one that is vastly superior to that of man.'[51]

Out-Of-Body Experiences and Consciousness

In out-of-body experience or OBE, a person's consciousness moves out of his body in certain situations, like accident, deep meditation or coma, and he can observe his body and other happenings from above with precision and clarity. It also involves the experience of altered consciousness like ecstasy, unconditional love, peace, higher wisdom, etc., Near-death experience or NDE is one type of OBE, which sometimes occurs at the time of clinical death of patients after a heart attack, coma, accident, etc., when the vital organs, such as the brain, are shut off.

There are hundreds of thousands of NDE cases reported with most having similar eternal experiences of unconditional love, an external view of the body and happenings near and away from the body with clarity; it also involves a meeting of consciousness or souls of departed relatives and friends, access of higher wisdom, positive change in perceptions, etc. Many have reported that their incurable diseases were cured without treatment after having undergone NDE. Dr Raymond Moody has conducted lots of studies on NDE and reported many cases.[52] Virginia University has been researching NDE and reincarnations for the last 50 years and contributed incontrovertible documentation of NDEs and reincarnations.

Two recent and popular cases of NDE are of Anita Moorjani and Dr Eben Alexander. Moorjani was suffering from fourth-stage cancer, and as per reports from her doctors, her vital organs were shutting down with only a few hours left to live as on 2 February 2006. After her NDE, she was cured of cancer naturally, much to the surprise of all, especially the medical community, and was discharged from the hospital in a few weeks. She has narrated the story in her bestselling book *Dying to Be Me*.[53] On that fateful day, her doctors told her family members that they could not do anything more, her vital organs had already shut down and she would not survive beyond the night. Her consciousness emerged out of the body; she writes that although her body was in a state of coma, she was clearly aware of everything, including her own body and what was happening around it, the sense of urgency and emotional frenzy expressed by others. But she was experiencing pure joy and jubilation. She was also aware of her husband and doctor speaking 40 feet away from the ICU, where the body was lying, and about her brother who was coming from their hometown thousands of kilometres away. She found everything beautiful, peaceful and calm, getting encompassed by pure and unconditional love, and felt being drawn away from the material surroundings. She felt a deep sense of freedom and liberation and was no longer restricted to the confines of space and time. She experienced the presence of her father and a close friend who had died 10 and three years ago, respectively. They communicated to her that her time had yet not come, and she was told to go back and live fearlessly. Then she opened her eyes and greeted everyone with a smile.

Doctors were surprised to hear the news, and when the duty doctor came to the ICU, she called him by name, though she had never met him. The doctor was shocked and asked her how she could recognize him, as she was in a coma when he had attended to her. She could even clearly narrate all the medical procedures the doctor had administered when she was in a coma. Immediately, a bone-marrow test was done, and no trace of cancer was found. Within five days, her tumours shrunk by 70 per cent, and she was released from the hospital after five weeks.

Dr Eben Alexander, a Harvard neurosurgeon with more than 20 years of experience, went into a coma for a week after severe E. coli meningitis with almost no chance of recovery. After an NDE and fast natural recovery, he shared this experience in his bestselling book, *Proof of Heaven*.[54]

He was infected by spontaneous E. coli bacterial meningitis, which can happen to only one in 10 million adults. With this chronic illness, initially, his recovery probability was 10 per cent and later nil. He was in a coma for a week, and his entire neocortex was shut down and inoperative. While in the coma, he experienced his consciousness moving out of his body, and had a visual experience of radiated fine filaments of white-gold light—he felt he was moving towards it. He experienced an ineffaceable extreme of purest, powerful and unconditional love. He experienced the presence of his sister, who had died a few years earlier. She communicated to him that he was always loved and cherished dearly, but his time had not come, and, eventually, he should go back—later, he opened his eyes. Then he completely recovered from his illness, including all his cognitive abilities.

Those who experience OBE also experience a paradigm shift in their perception that we are living pure consciousness or spiritual beings or souls with human experiences. But it is not essential to have OBE for achieving this paradigm shift. As said in Vedas, 'jnanayoga', the path of knowledge or wisdom, can help us achieve this goal. I am sure an open-minded reader can achieve this goal. Sceptics find some reasons and justifications to disbelieve OBE and NDE. But studies conducted by Dr Kenneth Ring and Sharon Cooper with respect to OBEs and NDEs of blind people, including people who were blind by birth and testified having seen and experienced many things inside the room and outside after clinical death or during OBE, are compelling evidence of consciousness and its survival after death as well as the fact that consciousness is not a product of the brain.[55] The above descriptions about mind, consciousness and mystical experiences, explanations of the scientists, especially the vivid and incontrovertible narrations of the above NDE experiences, and testimonies will help anybody attain the wisdom that they are living consciousness or spiritual beings with human experience. Nobel laureate Sir John Eccles, while conducting brain studies, recognized that we are spiritual beings with souls existing in the spiritual world as well as material beings with bodies and brains existing in a material world.[56]

In spite of all this, many people lead a life deprived of

the experience of this fundamental truth and wisdom, and live with a material and reductionist view, in a state of collective unconsciousness. It is mainly because of the widespread influence of material science and strong resistance of our ego-mind to change, which we need to address.

Science and Spirituality

Historically, science and spirituality, two vital aspects of life, were perceived as parallel lines. The division was cemented by Descartes's philosophy of dualism in the Cartesian split and the materialistic or reductionist approach of Newtonian physics. As scientific developments were based on the premises of Descartes and Newton, the spiritual aspect of human beings was taboo to most of the scientific community. Till the early nineteenth century, the (word) consciousness was not allowed to be used in scientific literature. Gradually, science accepted consciousness as reality and as the fundamental building block of everything in the universe. Fritz-Albert Popp, a German physicist, found in 1970s that all living things exist as constant tiny particles of light and maintained that this radiation is the true driving force that coordinates all cellular processes in the body.[57]

Quantum physics points to the existence of the zero-point field or energy—a sea of the energy field in which everything in the universe exists. 'Zero-point energy is a repository of all fields and ground energy states and all virtual particles—a field of fields.'[58]

Though science has only a faint idea about zero-point energy so far, physicists point out that the magnitude of this energy is unimaginable. To give some idea, famous physicist Richard Feynman said that this energy in one cubic meter of space is enough to boil all the oceans of the world.[59]

Though ancient spiritual traditions, right from the Vedas, spoke about this life force, there was no scientific validation. An important discovery of quantum mechanics is the non-locality of the atomic world, which has been proven by many studies, like that of Alain Aspect in Paris in 1982.[60] It showed that subatomic particles, like electrons, could influence another particle at the same time over any distance without the exchange of force or energy. It established the interconnectedness of everything in the universe; all are parts of one force, as told by spiritual traditions. This finding has shaken the basis of conventional physics. Another path-breaking finding was the observer effect—wave functions of subatomic particles can collapse and create matter at the intervention of the observer, giving a scientific explanation of creation.

Today we know that there exists a very delicate and precise pattern in every activity, whether it is at the quantum or cellular level or at the universal level, and neither science nor common sense has any idea about the superintelligence behind all these. Aristotle was one of the few who initially said that space was, in fact, a plenum. Michael Faraday pointed out, by the middle of the nineteenth century, that the most important aspect of energy was not the source but space around it and its influence on the other through some force.[61]

The first authentic study by Albert A. Michelson and Edward W. Morley in 1887 established the existence of the field of energy that permeates everything in the universe.[62] Many subsequent studies have substantiated this. Physicists gradually accepted this fact with the findings of Max Planck's study in 1911—the empty space was bursting with activity.[63] Einstein recognized it and said that the only fundamental reality was the underlying entity—the field itself.[64]

Recently, scientists have found that consciousness survives

the death of human beings. Despite various undeniable proofs of NDE and reincarnations, many authors and scientists hesitate to use terms like God or soul. Their approach may be correct as humanity has faced maximum violence or tortures and negativity in the name of God, and many are using God for vested interests and ego-mind gratifications when the truth is that God is beyond names and forms. So while associating this truth with a name, its meaning is limited to the label, which is counter-productive. One section of the scientists had apprehension of losing their credibility in the scientific community if terms like 'God' or 'soul' were used. But many reputed scientists considered it necessary to use the term 'God' to convey the truth. With the advancement of science, especially quantum mechanics, scientists have accepted concepts like individual consciousness, cosmic consciousness, unified energy field, zero-point energy; the scientific explanations of these concepts perfectly resemble the idea of God/soul, with only the terminologies being different. Bucke says that this sense of luminous field is one of the defining marks of cosmic consciousness.[65] Famous scientists, including Einstein, used the term 'soul' instead of 'consciousness' to refer to human beings' spiritual essence or entity. Einstein said, 'We are slowed down sound, and light waves, a walking bundle of frequencies turned into the cosmos. We are souls dressed up in sacred biochemical garments, and our bodies are the instruments through which our souls play their music.'[66] He also said, 'Synchronicity is God's way of remaining anonymous.' A review study conducted at the Cambridge Centre for Behavioral Studies notes, 'Brain-centered theories of consciousness seem to face inseparable difficulties.'[67]

All the religious and spiritual traditions, in general, teach us that the Almighty is the source of all creations, and human beings are a unique part of this force. This core idea was spoken of and explained in many ways; religions' goal was to make people aware of this fundamental truth. Most of the religions have drifted away from the core teachings towards practices and rituals. The power structures created by religions give importance to the dominance of religious heads or leaders; practices and rituals are given predominance over the core ideals and teachings; and practices of rituals have become an essential part of the egoic material world. This has hampered the spiritual development of the common masses, and the minds of the people were 'corrupted' with this collective unconsciousness leading to more and more conflicts and pain in life. Newtonian physics and Descartian philosophy added force to this materialistic or reductionist approach. Danah Zohar said, 'Newton's vision tore us out from the fabric of the universe.'[68] In the meanwhile, a new approach to spirituality with the support of science and spiritual science, has been emerging outside the boundaries of religions. It speaks about the basic religious ideals and teachings of all religions by using the language of science—that human being is a spiritual being with human experiences, which is part of the larger spiritual force. Quantum physics narrowed down the gap between the materialistic view and spiritual science; it teaches us that everything is energy (spirit) in different vibrations and frequencies.

Recent studies by Lynne McTaggart about the energy field underline the existence of a grand and unified energy field in which everything exists. The studies said, 'Human beings and all living things are a coalescence of energy in a field of energy connected to every other thing in the world. This pulsating energy field is the central engine of our being, and our consciousness, the alpha, and the omega of our existence.'[69] Hence Einstein said, '[...] The field is the only reality.' This field is responsible for all higher functions of our mind, source of information and body functions—even at the cellular level—and healing.

Goal of Life Becomes Clear

Now we are aware that we are much more than our bodies and minds; we are consciousness. Why are we not able to experience beingness or consciousness? Though we live within it, we are covered with a layer of the blockade and insulation of the ego-mind. This is a state of darkness or unconsciousness that can be removed only by the light of wisdom or awareness. It is clear that higher awareness of this truth is the true path towards achieving this goal for which we have to remove the blockade of the ego-mind. An in-depth awareness about the origin, development, function and strategies of the ego-mind (detailed in Chapter 7) will help us remove this blockade and move towards a state of awakening.

Observations on Materialist Views

Consciousness will continue to be a hard problem as long as materialist researchers try to find consciousness in the physical realm with physical research tools, as consciousness is not in the physical realm. Materialists do a lot of research on consciousness with a predetermined mind. In the material realm, you will not find the non-material field of energy with physical tools. Science does not accept the wisdom that has evolved from the contemplative research process and spiritual experiences over centuries. Such invaluable wisdom, available especially in the East, dates back thousands of years.

Quantum physics tells us that everything is energy at the subatomic level; all materials we perceive are energies in different frequency and vibration levels. Robert Hoss, a neuroscientist, said, 'Solid matter is just an illusion. At our most fundamental level, we may look something like this—an organized soup of subatomic particles popping in and out of existence within the infinite energy field of the Universe.'[70] Adi Shankara told us the universe is a '*maya*'.[71] So our perception that we experience the physical world outside is also an illusion. The basic principles of quantum physics are similar to many teachings of the Vedas in many respects. If science accepts such wisdom, human civilization will be benefitted immensely. Here Nikola Tesla's words are relevant: 'The day science begins to study non-physical phenomena, it will make more progress in one decade than in all the previous centuries of its existence.'

The reductionist approach, which believes that consciousness is a product of the brain, codified its findings and evolved a science of consciousness. In spite of decades-long researches, answers to basic questions as to how could brain or neuron activities produce subjective experiences and functions like thoughts, feelings, emotions attributing meaning to inputs, decisions, creativity, intentions, etc., which are not a function of a physical brain, could not be found. Conducting such researches will be like searching for a bird while being in water—with both being in different realms; the shadow of the bird might be caught in water, but neither a clear image nor the real bird will be.

6

CONSCIOUSNESS AND PRESENCE

The philosophies of Descartes and Newton divided the universe into two distinct aspects, i.e., mind and matter. Their basic premise was that the realm or area of matter belongs to science, the mind is a non-material part and science has nothing to do with it, and left it to the religions. Newtonian physics sees every object and its functions happening in space and time, including its interactions in the physical world, which can be measured and predicted. Newtonian physics had shown its limitations when quantum physics emerged and gathered momentum with the basic premise that everything is energy and interconnected. It tells about the immaterial world beyond space and time, a field of energy, information and immense potential; everything, including human beings, exists in consciousness. Rumi's words are relevant here, 'I have lived on the lip of insanity, wanting to know reasons, knocking on a door. It opens. I've been knocking from the inside.'

Presence, the Entry Point

Consciousness and presence are important pillars of spiritual science. We need to be fully aware of this truth, this reality, for the journey ahead towards awakening. To describe this truth, let us refer to a story.

One enlightened Zen master was walking through a jungle with his few disciples. The master remained a 100 per cent present and in an awakened state always. The disciples were eager to reach this level of presence.

One enthusiastic student asked him, 'Master, how can we enter this state, like you?'

The master remained quiet for a moment and then asked, 'Do you hear the sound of a waterfall?'

The student said, 'No.'

The master replied, 'That is the entry point.'

The student was confused, and after some time, he again asked the master, 'Master, suppose my answer was "yes, I can hear the sound of the waterfall", what would have been your answer then?'

The master said, 'The answer would be the same—that is the entry point.'

This story tells us that presence is the only entry point to the experience of our beingness.

But the attainment of presence is denied by the ego-mind in many ways; one, by generating continuous thoughts and emotions unabatedly without interruption. One thought arises every one-and-a-half second (approximate), with corresponding emotions and actions. This means that our mind is almost always disturbed, and we cannot fully focus our attention in the present moment. We have seen that most of these thoughts and emotions are negative, relating to past and future, and repetitive, which will trigger further thoughts in the same pattern. It means that our mind is always disturbed, and we are in the negative zone without being able to fully experience the present moment. It implies that the goal of focusing on and experiencing the present moment is not possible when our mind is disturbed. This great wisd from the Mahabharata. In an archery training session for the Pandavas and Karna, Guru om has been conveyed through a beautiful story Dronacharya kept a wooden fish on a tree near a pool and asked each one of them to aim at the fish, looking at the reflection in the water. While each was busy trying, the guru asked them, 'What are you seeing?' There were different answers—some saw the sky, some the tree and some the branches. When Arjuna's turn came, he said that he saw only the eye of the fish. When Dronacharya asked him to shoot, he was able to pierce the eye of the fish with his arrow. Here, the pool resembles the mind. If the mind is calm and clear without any disturbance of negative thoughts and emotions, we will be able to access and experience the goal (presence) and consciousness.

Another way ego-mind denies presence is by the way of interpreting sensory signals. We receive sensory signals every moment from the material world through our five senses that are registered in the mind. These make sense only after being interpreted by the ego-mind based on its perceptions. So the same signal may have different interpretations for different people. For example, the smell of an incense stick may be pleasant to those who used it during prayers in childhood. However, those who use it at the time of burial as per the customs in their culture, may experience the same signal as a very unpleasant one. Likewise, the ego-mind is always interpreting sensory signals based on the subconscious programme; in-depth experience of the present in an unbiased manner is the window to access 'beingness', which otherwise is obliterated by the ego-mind.

Present

Present means here and now. We have seen that we live in an illusion of the past–present–future continuum in the linear physical world. We believe that the past-present-future continuum is a reality. The truth is that only the present is the reality; past and future are non-existent, unreal, and so, illusions. Initially, some may have doubts. As the present moment is the entry point to the state of awakening, we need to be fully aware of it.

Are past and future real? Anything real exists only now; we can access it either directly or indirectly, pay attention to it and experience it. Some may think that we are able to pay attention to the past or future. No, we are only remembering the past and anticipating the future. Can we live in the past or future? No. Can we experience anything in the past or future? No. We can only remember the past and anticipate, visualize or plan for the future, and when does that planning or visualization happen? It happens now, in the present. We can live, do and experience anything only in the present moment. The present is the only reality. So far, we were living our lives, indulging in thoughts, emotions and activities, believing that past and future are real, especially the immediate past and future; almost all our thoughts, feelings and actions are related to the past and future, which means we are living in the past or future in an illusory manner all the time.

Of course, past and future are important to living in the physical world, but both have only limited relevance. The past has lots of data, information and experience, which we can use to enrich the present moment and plan for the future. But the planning happens only in the present. As we can only live in the present moment, the synonym of life is present or now.

All our problems and sufferings arise when our lives are driven by the ego-mind related to the past and future. It is our life's goal to deepen our awareness of the now and live a life fully anchored in the present moment. The quality of life depends on the extent and quality of our presence. We can approach and access our beingness, our true self, only through the window of the present moment. Ego-mind exists only when we live relating with the past and future, and it loses its control over us when we are in the present. On the other hand, all the ego-mind's strategies are aimed at denying us the present moment. As our life had been driven by the ego-mind so far, the space or window of the present has been reduced to become very narrow or practically nil. This was because the ego-mind was developed and surviving on the illusion of the past and future; any awareness of the present moment reality and access to it meant a threat to the existence of the ego-mind and its control on us.

The awareness of this truth that the present moment is the only reality is the starting point to our awakening process because awakening can happen and be experienced only in the present moment; to what extent the awakening happens depends upon our level of awareness. In the egoic physical world, many people are uneasy and uncomfortable when there is nothing to do in the present. We are not aware that the ego-mind has developed an addictive and compulsive tendency to remain engaged in activities relating to the past or future. If we have a few minutes of free time, we immediately get into unnecessary linear activities, which have relevance to the past or future, like scanning WhatsApp messages, Facebook posts, repeated newscasts, etc. This shows our addictive tendency to go into the past, revisit what happened, emotionally react to it, and feel anxious wondering what all is going to happen. This is how we lose the experience of the present moment, which is the reality, the life.

Ego-mind has created another illusion that the immediate past and future are real to justify our emotional reactions and deny the present. For example, a parent is angry with a child for being naughty. The question is whether the parent will be angry about something the child did a year ago? No, because his rationality prevails over the ego-mind with the thought that the child was being naughty a year ago and that happened in the past, and is not existent or real now. He would understand that any emotional reaction to something unreal is unconsciousness or foolishness. An incident that took place mere five minutes ago is also a thing of the past and hence unreal. Is it not? So it is unconscious to react emotionally to the immediate past or even future.

Another illusion of the ego-mind is that the immediate future is perceived as real; for example, a student waiting for the exam is not anxious six months before the results are to be announced. The ego-mind creates anxiety and the emotional reaction for the immediate future, say, one day before or a few hours before the announcement of the results.

In both examples, emotional reactions are either to the immediate past or future due to the illusion created by the ego-mind that the immediate past and future are real and existing in order to deny us presence and rational response. This higher awareness will gradually reduce this tendency and help us come out of this pattern and remain more focussed in the present with rational responses to different life situations. This will help us change our subconscious behavioural patterns and improve our quality of life substantially.

Deepening Presence through Sensory Perceptions

As the present is the entry point to experiencing our beingness, it is vital for us to be deeply aware of it. We experience the present primarily through sensory experiences; sometimes a deeper presence is felt through the experience of the 'isness' itself. Sensory experiences mean experiences through five senses: vision, sound, touch, smell and taste. Another tactic that ego-mind uses with us is that it reduces our ability to pay complete attention to and experience sensory perceptions. The quality of experience of anything depends upon the quality of attention we are giving to it.

Nature has given us the ability to be fully in the present and have deeper sensory perceptions. The quality of our presence and attention depends on the space we are creating in the background of something we are paying attention to. Once Michelangelo was carving a marble statue, and a bystander expressed his astonishment and asked, 'How could you do that?' He replied, 'The statue is already there within the marble block; I am only removing the unwanted portions.' The existence of every material item and our perception of it is possible when there is space around it. A statue emerges when space is created around it. So the higher goal of life is to carve out the present moment from past-present-future linearity by creating space before and after the present moment; be in the present moment fully with whatever activities you are engaged in. Realize the truth and secret that the present moment is independent of past and future, and it exists in isolation. You can experience this present as an independent moment in isolation, which would be the state of awakening.

Children usually pay full attention to the things they are interested in. For example, when we see a colourful fish in an aquarium, we may only see it casually, like seeing a picture in two dimension. But when a child sees this fish, he is fully present in the moment and sees it with 100 per cent attention to its three-dimensionality, taking in the experience. With mind engineering wisdom and practice, our sensory experiences become spiritual experiences. Practising this higher wisdom will gradually enhance the quality of experiences, the experience of beingness in every object, and the experience of presence at a deeper level, which is the state of awakening.

In order to improve the quality of life and move ahead towards awakening, we need to create more space for presence and deepen our sensory experiences.

Vision

Have you seen how children look at the things they are interested in? A child may forget everything when he looks at a colourful fish for the first time in an aquarium, leaving behind any sense of time or space. He is in a timeless dimension, 100 per cent present, looking at the fish without any judgement or prejudice or preconceived notion. When we grow up, we lose such higher qualities due to the interference of our ego-mind to deflect our attention from the present moment, reality and experience.

Sound

Sound also exists when there is silence in the background, just like material things can be experienced when there is space around them. When we hear a sound with an awareness of the background silence and give selective attention to it, it is not only a spiritual experience but also a mental exercise to sharpen our cognitive ability and enhance our quality of life.

For example, while listening to a song, we are able to segregate the sound of the singer from the medley of different musical instruments, which enhances our experience of hearing the song. Through this practice, students can improve their concentration and cognitive abilities. Usually, we are not able to listen to speeches or talks with full attention due to distractions caused by the ego-mind. In order to deepen the listening experience, mentally reciting what is being heard or visualizing the ideas or the meanings of what has been said will give more depth and help us remain fully present without distractions.

Taste, smell and touch sensations

Usually, when we have these sensory experiences, our attention and thoughts wander somewhere else, due to which the quality of these sensory experiences is minimized. For example, many people eat while being engaged in a lot of activities, like watching TV, attending to phone call, etc., and they are not able to enjoy the food at all. Full attention and awareness regarding the food we are consuming is essential for enjoying it, producing sufficient digestive enzymes and making the body alert to use the calories and nutrients. Similarly, we also need to have a higher awareness of the sensory experiences of smell and touch sensation for a better quality of life. The whole body and mind should be involved in the process of doing different activities; the whole body should experience the thrill of these sensory experiences. Doing so would mean that our body and mind are aligned with the present moment.

When we are totally present while experiencing sensory signals, the corresponding processing areas in the brain become fully activated. Such experiences result in the restructuring of our brain circuits in a healthy manner, weakening the habitual negative patterns and its circuits.

Refining Presence

A person's success depends upon how far he is liberated from various illusions and unconsciousness, which the ego-mind makes us believe. We have seen that the perception and beliefs of the subconscious mind are deep-rooted, and we are not aware of it usually—it works like autopilot. The most fundamental illusion we have is a continuum of past-present-future, which means we are under the illusion that the present moment itself does not have an existence and relevance. The truth is just the opposite; the present moment is the only reality; past and future are non-existent. As it is a deep-rooted illusion based on which the ego-mind survives, it is difficult to become aware of the truth and reality of the present.

With higher awareness and practice, we can gradually break free from these tendencies and use them as the means for being in the present. The basic thing the ego-mind does is that it creates 'mind chatter' or a chain of thoughts. When there is some thought in mind, we are not able to give full attention to any other thing. So becoming aware of those thoughts and paying attention to those becomes an experience of the present moment. It will help us create space between the thoughts and help us reduce its number, its compulsive pattern and remain more in the present. Negative thoughts create corresponding negative emotions in different degrees. Sometimes, it is mild, creating feelings of unease and irritation, which is considered normal. But every negative emotion correlates with the past or future, preventing us from remaining in the present.

The quality of our life depends on the quality of our experiences. The quality of our experiences depends on the degree of attention and awareness we are bringing to it; we can give full attention only when we are 100 per cent present. The quality of our activities, efficiency and effectiveness in any field will be of much higher order when we do it being fully present. Training children to be able to do so can help in enhancing their cognitive abilities substantially. Not only can we bring in more awareness and attention to structured activities or in formal set-ups like offices, we can also bring in higher awareness and attention to our smallest of activities, and have a higher quality of life rooted in presence.

For example, while getting up in the morning, we can bring awareness to our state of body, mind, chain of thoughts, breathing patterns, and start the day with a few deep mindful breaths and positive resolutions. Such mindfulness practices every waking moment help avoid negative and wandering thoughts. It is reported that 47 per cent of our activities are mechanical or routine without application of the mind, which means that we are not in the present at all about half the time.[1] When deeper awareness is brought into every part of the body and the smallest of activities, the entire body will respond in a healthy and positive way, and all our activities will manifest our beingness, an awakened state.

While sitting idle, even in a natural environment like a park or seashore, our mind usually wanders. A wandering mind is a negative mind. Due to wandering thoughts, the entire brain becomes active; when we focus on specific activities, only the corresponding area in the brain is activated, and the other parts get rest. Some situations, like sitting in a park or seashore, can be an experience of higher awareness and total presence if we pay full unbiased attention to things like a flower, tree or waves.

Linearity of Time: A Deep-Rooted Illusion

The concept of time and its linearity are a deep-rooted unconsciousness or illusion developed and carried on for many centuries. This illusion is a stumbling block in becoming aware of and experiencing presence. Hence, it requires deep dive into this aspect for higher awareness and becoming aware of the reality of timelessness, 'isness' or 'suchness' (as Buddhists say). This higher awareness and conviction is a requirement for progress in the journey towards awakening.

We all have a notion that time is precious, and we live in a world governed by time. Time is perceived with reference to its units like a second or minute or hours. When we talk about a particular duration of time, it is measured from now onwards (future) or backwards from the present moment (past). In the spiritual sense, we are aware that past and future are non-existent, and hence time is an illusion, and only the present moment timelessness is a reality that exists in isolation from the past and future. This awareness is of higher order and contrary to the illusion we have had over many centuries.

As our life is driven by the ego-mind, we make sense of everything in the physical world relating to the past or future. Hence, we use time units frequently for various practical purposes. But we should not be stuck at this point. When nature envisages human beings to evolve spiritually, and when we are aware that we are spiritual beings with human experiences, we have to live in reality, i.e., in the present, which is the entry point to this experience of beingness.

How the Present Is Denied by the Ego-Mind

We are aware that the present is the reality that exists in isolation, and it is the ego-mind's strategy to deny us the experience of the present. Based on the nature of perceptions and beliefs of the subconscious mind, it has developed corresponding needs to be fulfilled. The ego-mind always has some needs and desires to be fulfilled in future, which means that a person controlled to a great extent by the ego-mind is never fully in the present. For example, a person hurt or neglected in childhood might develop the thought process in their subconscious mind that he needs to remain aloof or avoid social interactions, and his mind will always be preoccupied with thoughts, feelings and ideas on how to avoid interaction with others. On the other hand, as the ego-mind has addictive tendency to have pain, such people, in some instances, seek attention and appreciation from others, getting insulted or neglected in return. This way the ego-mind ensures that they remain in conflict and pain, denying the experience of the present moment.

Present Moment Exists in Isolation

We have seen that everything happens only in the present moment, and past and future have a limited relevance in life. In order to free us from the deep-rooted illusion of time, or past and future, and deepen our awareness, let us see a few examples.

Suppose you are sitting on a bench by the roadside, watching and fully experiencing a beautiful garden (presence) across the road, and the sight is being rarely obstructed by moving people. After some time, the number of people walking on the road increases, disturbing the sight and experience. After some time, a procession begins, and the view of the garden is reduced further. After a while, the number of people in procession increases, due to which the experience of the garden becomes almost nil. This is what happens to us in life and our mind as we grow up; the number of thoughts gradually increases from childhood, and become a continuous chain of thoughts when we turn older. Due to the latter, we are able to have a glimpse of the magnificence of the present moment only rarely. We have to reverse the pattern with higher awareness and close observation of thoughts, which will provide space between thoughts—and gradually we will be able to experience the beauty and power of presence more and more.

The following example clearly shows us the illusion of linearity or past-present-future continuum and the existence of the present moment in isolation. Suppose we are standing by a seashore, watching and enjoying the sea waves for one hour. We believe that we have been enjoying the view of the sea and the waves for the past one hour. The reality is we are watching and experiencing only the 'present' wave approaching us. Are we enjoying the previous wave? No. It does not exist, but we do have the information and memory of the previous wave (past). Can we enjoy the next wave now (future)? No. But based on the experience of the last wave (past), we can position ourselves and plan to experience the next wave (future) fully, and the planning also takes place only in the present moment. We can only enjoy and experience the present wave (present moment). That will be independent of past and future waves.

This is the way life is. Before having this higher awareness, we were under the influence of the illusion that we were enjoying the waves for one hour, which is not true. The awareness that the present moment is only the reality, independent and exists in isolation is of very high order and capable of making a major shift in awareness that moves us closer to awakening.

Our goal is a better quality of life. We live only in the present moment or now, so now is the synonym of life. As prudent people, we should have a concern about our life or present moment; we should ask ourselves as frequently as we can, 'Am I fully in the present?' This alertness itself opens up the window of present-moment awareness, activates the faculty of focusing our attention selectively and facilitates full experiences of the present moment reality.

Present: The Reality

We are powerful, perfect and whole when we are fully in the present moment. The present moment is in isolation, precious, whole, with nothing lacking. The ego-mind, like a radar, waits for some signals, so that it can easily justify emotional reactions and deny us presence. The deep awareness of the fundamental truth and reality that the present moment exists in isolation, as a whole without any lack, is essential. As the present moment 'is', it is whole, complete and we have to accept this reality. We cannot change it; the way we look at the present moment, world, others and life situations has to change.

Similarly, the way we see the outside world and react is as per our perception, beliefs and our image created by the ego-mind. When we have the higher awareness that we are consciousness, spiritual beings (part of a larger consciousness), whole, complete, powerful in the moment and do not lack anything in the now, then what prevents us from being fully happy and peaceful in the present moment? In this moment, most of us are not happy and peaceful. If we are introspecting in an unbiased manner, we find that most of us are unhappy without any reason in the present moment or now. What do we do when we are in a happy moment? Don't we smile, sing and dance? Why can't we do it now? All the problems or negative thoughts we are having are not relevant in the present moment—they are related to the past, future and to what others think, which the ego-mind is bringing in with some justifications with a view to deny us the present. Of course, some might have adverse life situations or illnesses; naturally, they cannot sing and dance; instead of emotional reactions, accepting the reality and rationally responding to it will empower and strengthen us to face such situations in a much better way. Some spiritually evolved people use such situations to shed away the ego-mind-created images and increase the experience of presence, which is a powerful spiritual experience, and state of awakening.

What is present is reality, what is reality is present. We can experience something that we are aware of and paying attention to. Our quality of life depends on the quality of our experiences in the present. As the ego-mind is preventing the experience of our reality, consciousness, presence and higher quality of life, we need to have deeper awareness about the ego-mind. This higher awareness will strengthen and enable us to break free from its control.

7
ORIGIN, GROWTH AND OPERATION OF THE EGO-MIND

Cell biologists say that our brains are naturally structured to be happy. We have about 40 trillion cells in our body, and their basic nature is to live in harmony and peace. Each cell takes part in all our body functions, and lives like 40 trillion organisms co-existing in harmony. When faced with negative emotions, cells activate their defense mechanisms and shift to protection mode from growth mode; when in the protection mode, the cells are in an unhealthy state.

We are part of one reality or force and hence are equals in the spiritual context. Separateness is the opposite of intimacy, connectedness or treating everyone as equals. But the ego-mind gives a different picture; the ego-mind perceives everyone as either superior or inferior, not equals, so that separateness is maintained, and conflicts are ensured.

The ego-mind is a living non-physical entity that drives our lives, and it is our enemy or the great wall that blocks our access and experience of the present and our true essence, the consciousness. We need to become aware of all the aspects of the ego-mind—how it originated, survived, grew, strengthened and is being operated; once we have this awareness, the ego-mind will be totally exposed and weakened, and it will lose its control over us. We will not be identified further with it. When we become aware of all its strategies, we will not fall prey to it, and gradually free ourselves from the control of the ego-mind, and access and experience the consciousness—that would be the state of awakening.

Origin of the Ego-Mind

It is tough to take our attention to a higher awareness of consciousness from the body and mind identity levels, as we are addictively identified with the ego-mind. From childhood, we identify with our physique and name (body consciousness), and we have seen children saying something like 'Sunny is playing' when they are referring to the physique/body, and the body identity is expressed in this manner. When we reach adulthood, we start identifying with images, roles, names, forms, perceptions, beliefs, and in short, the image created by the ego-mind.

How Is Ego-Mind Developed?

As this is very important in the process of transformation or awakening, we need to get into it deeply. Nature has given a defense mechanism to every creature on Earth for its survival. The human newborn is too vulnerable and dependent; it needs support, help and care of parents or caregivers for essentials, like food, protection and shelter, for its survival. When a child is born, it is only body-conscious. An infant's defense mechanism is operated through the manifestation of emotions; when there is any need for the essentials of survival or when it faces any threat, it expresses emotions, like fear, sadness, etc., depending upon the nature of the need or life situation. Other than body survival, infants have no name, role or image to protect. Children perceive each experience as it is felt, understood, made sense, and conclusions are drawn based on the experiences, which become their perceptions and belief systems. Children up to the age of about seven have brains with theta waves and do not have the analytical ability to understand the rationale or intentions behind various interactions and experiences. Every experience coupled with corresponding emotion is stored in the subconscious mind, along with the meaning attributed to it. So the repeated experiences up to the age of about seven result in drawing corresponding conclusions about self, others, life situations and the world outside.

For example, a child frequently scolded may draw a conclusion that 'I am not up to the mark' or 'I am inferior to others', which he may manifest throughout his entire life as an introvert and become a less confident person. His conclusion is not necessarily true; his parent's intention to correct him might not have been understood by him. But whatever has been experienced and felt has been recorded in his mind. The sum total of these conclusions creates an overall image of him and becomes the foundation of his personality. These perceptions and beliefs function as a default 'computer programme'.

In the normal course, a person is not aware of the perceptions and beliefs that drive his life. Within a couple of years after birth, a child gets a name, and he starts identifying with the name. Gradually when he grows up and undergoes similar emotional experiences, he reinforces the perceptions, beliefs and corresponding neuronal circuits. While he gradually grows up, he may get assigned many roles, like a son, an executive, a father or a businessman, and his conscious mind would be aware of it. The sum total of one's conclusions, beliefs, perceptions and image formed up to the age of seven becomes the subconscious programme that will be manifested without awareness in later part of life through names, roles and images. A person identifies with all these images of the ego-mind—'I' means the ego-mind created image—and he shifts predominant consciousness from the body to ego-mind consciousness or identity.

Children do not have a sense of doubt about the signals, perceptions and experiences. So their perceptions become their belief, and that becomes their reality later in life. The perceptions of parents, teachers and other caregivers influence children's perceptions and beliefs to a great extent. So, they play a huge role in moulding the personality of children. Even very young children have great observation power, including the ability to feel others' emotions with the help of their mirror hormones. Some studies show that even a foetus has emotional experiences and is influenced by its mother's feelings and emotions, so pregnant women need to have a positive and healthy state of mind.[1] All these childhood experiences become part of their subconscious mind, which drives most of their thoughts, feelings and actions in response to life situations. This is the reason why people follow a certain pattern while reacting emotionally in different life situations. For example, a person who is angry frequently, despite his conscious mind being aware that this pattern of behaviour is not healthy, is not able to change it in the normal course. Similarly, many people resort to various activities, like taking healthy and organic food, supplements, doing exercises, body care activities, yoga, wellness programmes, etc., as the conscious mind wants to have a healthy body and mind, but the results may not be as expected, as nature of thoughts based on beliefs and perceptions of subconscious mind supersede the conscious mind. Cells in our body may respond positively to such activities, but it will be superseded by the biochemistry driven by our subconscious mind. For example, histamine promotes the immune system and triggers cells in a positive and healthy manner. However, the signals sent by the brain/mind to other parts of the body trigger the cells to supersede the local effect of histamine. The brain produces such substances in accordance with the perceptions and beliefs of the subconscious mind. When the mind is stressed, the adrenaline produced overrides cell functions in other parts of the body, nullifying the effect of histamine. We can put it in another example: our efforts to have good health without changing the subconscious programme is like cleaning a water stream without stopping the discharge of toxic substances at the source of the water stream.

Strengthening of the Ego-Mind

Nature envisages that human beings have a happy and healthy life. The quality of life experiences of children is of a higher order; in the normal course, they are playful, fully present, happy, healthy, creative, inquisitive, loving, not worried about the past or anxious about the future; in a way, they live in the present and positive zone. By nature, adults' brains want to have new and positive experiences, and the brain undergoes fast circuitry changes when there are new experiences than the routine negative experiences. The neocortex and PFC, which are the processing areas of higher consciousness and spiritual experiences, mature in the latter part of the 20s. This means that nature envisages human beings to evolve spiritually and gradually after the emotional spell of teenage years and early period of adulthood.

But with the development of a civilization based on materialism, linearity and self-centeredness over many generations, we follow an ego-driven life addicted to the materialistic linear world. The ego-mind is a strong entity processed mainly in the left hemisphere of the brain. Some scientists are of the view that the processing capacity of this brain area is one million times stronger than the brain area that processes the true self or consciousness.[2] This situation has denied the natural spiritual development and awakening amongst us. The materialistic linear world and our ego-minds are complementary to each other and are parts of a vicious circle. As this has become a common phenomenon, it has been considered natural development—conflict and suffering are considered normal, seen as facilitating further strengthening of the ego-mind.

Nature of the Ego-Mind

The basic nature of the ego-mind comprises fear, pain and a sense of lack in different forms; it operates with an addictive and compulsive pattern of thoughts, emotions and behaviour. The neurological processor of the ego-mind is the left hemisphere of the brain, which is logical in nature. So the people involved in activities or careers connected more with language, technical field, mathematics, etc., are more prone to have a strong ego-mind. In today's world, the majority of the so-called intelligentsia falls within this category.

The material world in which we live is linear, and everything is made sense of by relating it to the past and future. For example, when we are watching a movie, the scene we are witnessing in the present moment is relevant or is made sense of by relating it with the past and the anticipated future. The ego-mind also exists by relating to the past and future, and, in this context, the outside linear world is the egoic world, and the ego-mind has a tendency to be addictively engaged to the outside physical world and the occurring events. The ego-mind has no control on us when we are entirely in the present moment. Hence, if there is some free time, people will have a tendency to get engaged in compulsive and addictive activities of the linear world rather than meditating briefly or undertaking simple practices, like observing their breathing pattern or thoughts or emotions, or experiencing the present moment fully, which enables us to move away from the ego-mind world to the doors of presence and beingness.

Fear

The basic emotion of the ego-mind is fear, and this is the primordial negative emotion. We have seen that every organism on Earth has a defense mechanism for survival, and when there is a threat to survival, their defense mechanism comes into effect. The urge for survival is naturally deep-rooted in every living creature. As a human infant is dependent on others for survival, it senses threat to survival, which causes fear of death. This is the most deep-rooted negative emotion. All other negative emotions have some element of fear involved in it. Nature has given us the defense mechanism to face the challenges and threats to the survival of our bodies.

As we grow, we get identified with names, roles, images, forms, the ego-mind-made false self, and we trigger the defense mechanism for the protection and survival of our ego-mind image, which nature does not envisage. The ego-mind is under constant threat of survival and fear, though it shows up as strong. When a defense mechanism is in operation, we are under stress and strain, and since our bodies are not compatible with long-term stress, it results in many illnesses and other adverse consequences.

Sense of lack

Another basic nature of the ego-mind is a sense of lack. This trait is manifested by a sense of incompleteness or craving for more and more in everything. As we all identify with the ego-mind, we have a craving for higher positions, richness, possessions, name, fame, specific life situations, and so on to different degrees, depending on the nature and density of the ego-mind. This nature of the ego-mind is manifested consciously and unconsciously. Due to this, there is always a sense of lack in life when compared to others, and it rarely gets fulfilled. It is like a bottomless pit, and this is the basic nature of the ego-mind. At the unconscious level, this is part of the subconscious belief that one experiences in childhood. Every child has a lot of unfulfilled desires and needs in childhood. When a child is unable to fulfill their desires early in life, negative conclusions are drawn, like, 'I am not up to the mark' or 'something is lacking in me', etc. These conclusions are carried on throughout their life and manifested as a sense of lack or incompleteness without their awareness. This always makes the child crave and wish for material things or seek mental satisfactions, which never gets fulfilled completely.

When our one need is fulfilled, the feeling of fulfilment is short-lived, and the ego-mind starts searching for other needs to be fulfilled. There is no point in time when ego-mind does not have a need to be fulfilled. This state of mind helps the ego-mind to be in the projected future for fulfilment and not in the present. One can be contended only in the present moment, not in the future. So this is another strategy of the ego-mind to deny us the present moment. This sense of lack spreads to all aspects of life. Some people develop a craving for food and never get satisfied. This tendency sometimes develops into a mental disorder called bulimia.

Separateness

A deep sense of separateness is a basic nature of the ego-mind. It ensures conflict, pain and the existence of ego-driven patterns in our lives. This is experienced at two levels.

i. When we identify with the ego-mind, it means that we are not aware of, accessing and experiencing our true essence, consciousness. The ego-mind ensures that we maintain this separateness from our core, our essence, for its own survival.
ii. Separateness also implies the absence of cordiality with others or not treating others as equals and part of one reality or force. The ego-mind wants to maintain this position so that conflict and pain become a regular feature, and the ego-mind is strengthened. The ego-mind deploys various strategies for this purpose.

Separateness and Conflict

We are part of one larger entity, and we are all intimately and intricately connected. When we are part of one larger entity, there is no room for ill will or negative thinking or emotions against others or conflicts. To put it in an example, it is like one finger having ill will and conflict with other fingers, and trying to harm each other. When the whole palm is shown in a mirror, fingers become aware that all are part of the same entity or source, and one finger harming another is equal to harming itself.

Most of the time, we are engaged in having unnecessary negative thoughts about others, creating many conflicts and suffering, which result in denying us happiness and wellness. More than 50 per cent of our thoughts are related to the following:

i. I want to please others and create a good impression on others.
ii. I want attention, appreciation and recognition from others, or

iii Ill will about others due to our ego-based perceptions of others in different life situations.

Now we realize that all these negative thoughts and emotions involving others are due to unconsciousness or the lack of proper awareness that we are spiritual beings and part of the same reality. It harms us in many ways. So, let us put an end to it.

Conflict and Pain

As the ego-mind needs frequent conflicts and pain, it uses many strategies and illusions, and follows addictive tendencies that become part of our behavioural patterns. This may be rigid in people with rigid ego-mind, who create frequent conflicts and pains. These patterns are part of the subconscious mind programme, and we are not aware of their origin and the way they operate. So, it is necessary to become aware of how these programmes have been made in childhood and the life situations that led to this programming in an unbiased manner. This wisdom is an essential and emergency need, as lots of conflicts occur in our everyday lives. Such tendencies are manifested more when the subconscious mind is active in informal life situations, especially in those involving families. In formal situations and interactions, there are certain norms and decorum to be followed, so the manifestation of conflicts is less, as the conscious mind is active. There is no compulsion of norms in informal life situations and, hence, the subconscious mind manifests its programme freely. Its need to create conflicts and pain is frequently manifested through behavioural patterns.

Ego-Mind and Stress

Nature has all the checks and balances in every aspect of life on Earth. For example, nature envisages that human beings need to face threatening and challenging situations in life. A defense mechanism is in place for it; for example, a person facing a lion needs to be stressed. The hypothalamus-pituitary-adrenal axis has a mechanism to produce and send adrenaline signals to all parts of the body, activating the flight or fight mode by triggering many biophysical functions, like constricting the blood vessels for pumping more blood to muscles, generating more glucose, energy, etc. Other bodily functions are paused to prepare the mind and body to be able to fully face such a challenge.

Neuroscientists say that short-term stresses are not much harmful to the body. But the problem is that as we have developed a strong ego-mind and started identifying with it. 'I' means the image of the ego-mind, and we trigger the same defense mechanism and create stress when there is a threat to our ego-mind-created image. The experience of this kind of threat to the ego-mind and the stressful situations continue daily for a long period, which is not envisaged by nature. The prolonged stress and production of stress hormones are harmful for the body. As per modern medical science, most of the diseases are in some way connected with prolonged stress in life. It is found that about 170 genes are affected by stress, out of which 100 are directly fully shut off, most of them being related to the production of proteins of healing.[3]

Ego-Mind and Conflicts

The dominance of the subconscious mind over our conscious mind is always visible in human relationships. For example, young people fall in love or marry and plan a romantic or heavenly life; it is also said that marriages takes place in heaven. But many people, especially couples from the current generation, experience a lot of conflicts in their relationship, resulting in many emotional problems, as they are more dominated by their left brain and are emotional in nature. Their ego-mind starts dominating and manifesting after some time.

Rigid Ego-Mind

We have seen that about 95 per cent of our thoughts, emotions and activities in life are driven by our subconscious mind. This is an average estimate, and in many cases of rigid ego-mind, the percentage is higher; many are close to 100 per cent, and the problem with such people is that they are not even aware of their identification with the ego-mind, the conflict and the pain it creates, and the toll it takes on life. On the one hand, they are not aware of it, and, on the other hand, the ego-mind strongly resists any new wisdom to change or transform. They and the people around them are real sufferers. They also usually refuse the assistance of other people to bring in more awareness or opportunities for change. When people are fully identified with ego-mind, they are taken over by the ego-mind. Many of them would likely be suffering from psychic disorders or illnesses at a later stage.

Arrogance of the Ego-Mind

Arrogance is the opposite of simplicity or humility. When our ego-mind grows in strength, the resistance to change develops to a sense of arrogance. A dense ego-mind will have a strong sense of arrogance. The arrogance is manifested in three ways.

i. **Absence of open-mindedness to any new knowledge or wisdom and tendency to stick to the ego-mind's patterns, beliefs and perceptions:** Due to the lack of open-mindedness, the dense ego-mind tends to come to an immediate conclusion and judgement in different life situations. Judgemental attitude, even including positive judgements like 'good' to new knowledge, restricts learning process and awareness. What matters is how much awareness one can get at the experiential level.

ii. **Absence of humility to admit one's limitations:** Human intellect has a lot of limitations in understanding the mysteries of the universe. Even advanced science has very limited knowledge, be it about a tiny atom or a cell or the vast universe. Usually, our ego-mind does not admit to these limitations and holds an attitude of 'I know everything', which helps it to avoid new wisdom for change.

iii. **Denial of mistakes:** Even when wrong and harmful, the dense ego-mind never admits its mistakes and always tries to justify how it thinks, feels and manifests. It is very difficult for a person with a dense ego-mind to say 'sorry' for any of his wrong actions.

Defense of the Ego-Mind

The ego-mind always fears for its existence because its foundation is weak and unreal or based on illusions like past and future. For clarity, let us understand this point using a metaphor. Imagine that a human statue made of ice has life, and it believes that it is very strong. But its existence will always be threatened and it will fear for its survival, as its strength will be an illusion since even the slight heat of the sun or temperature change will be a threat to its survival. Similarly, though it seems stronger, the ego-mind is under constant threat of being exposed to reality with higher awareness and new experiences. So our ego-mind adopts various strategies for its survival. We know that the best defense is offense or aggression. The ego-mind adopts a strategy by trying to control others or the situations so that it remains safe. The ego-mind is afraid of new experiences and changes as those would weaken its position. Hence, we can see that the tendency to control others and resistance to change is directly proportional to the density or hardness of ego-mind. When the ego-mind is in control of others and situations, it ensures that the situations are routine and linear in the time dimension, i.e., related to past and future, so that any change is resisted effectively.

The Love between Egoic People

We have seen the basic nature of consciousness—it is love, peace and joy. Though we know its meaning in common parlance, we need to reflect more on love as it has many dimensions. As the basic nature of ego-mind—fear, sense of lack and separateness— is the opposite of true love, the ego-mind has its strategies to deny the experience of true love. Ego-mind 'loves' opposites of love—conflicts, fear and emotional pain. But it likes or 'loves' favourable life situations and people as per the perception, belief and needs of the ego-mind or as long as it serves the purpose of the ego-mind. So the love of the ego-mind is conditional and shallow. Love towards a person can easily turn into conflict as per the patterns of the ego-mind. A person with true love first loves himself deeply, but a person identified with a dense ego-mind does not love himself. So he is interested in creating conflict and pain for himself, which has adverse consequences on his health and wellness. When we are driven by the ego-mind, our sense of love towards ourselves is fake, we are engaged in thoughts, emotions and activities, which are harmful to us and others, in every moment. An egoic person's conscious mind wants to interact with others with love, but it happens rarely and superficially in reality. It is difficult for them to have deep unconditional love, intimacy and manifestations of love, like compassion, forgiveness, apologetic regret, oneness with others, sharing attitude, etc. Attempts of the conscious mind will be overpowered by the subconscious mind of the dense ego-mind, which is the reason for most of the conflicts between couples, families and many groups in society.

Love of Awakened People

Spiritually evolved or awakened people are aware that they are spiritual beings or consciousness, and their basic nature is love of a higher quality, unconditional love. As we are part of the divinity, which is unconditional love, our basic nature is this love of a higher order, and the experience of this true love and its manifestation is the ultimate goal, the awakened state. When we stay true to this basic nature, all our activities and experiences will be of a higher quality, benefitting not just us but others around us too. A person walking with a candle in the night spreads light for others too.

When love is our basic nature, life will be a free flow without conflicts and pains. All problems and conflicts in life arising from human interactions are due to the absence of true love. We are naturally oriented to live in love and harmony. When we are driven by consciousness or love, our body and mind are in the healthiest state. If there is true love, there is no room for conflicts and pain.

Ego-Mind and Tendency to Control

Another strategy the ego-mind adopts to avoid change in beliefs is by protecting its mental positions. This is manifested by exercising power or control over others. This tendency can be observed in all spheres of life—be it in family, workplace or social interactions. In the workplace, a boss with a dense ego-mind wants to micromanage the subordinates without giving room for using their creativity, innovativeness and abilities. Instructions from such bosses will be not only 'what to do', but 'how to do' in detail, which is an indication of their rigid ego-mind. Such situations are bound to not be cordial. In families, some ego-minded parents exercise excess control over children over every little thing, by telling them what to do, what not to do, how to do it, without giving them an opportunity to use their abilities and creative thinking. This is a dangerous tendency with a lot of consequences. Children have a tremendous amount of creativity, inquisitiveness, innovativeness and skill in handling delicate activities. They need to be encouraged by parents for their personalities to bloom or 'flower' and for them to become efficient, competent, effective and confident people in the future. It is seen that children who were excessively controlled by parents do not develop independent thinking, and there are chances of them becoming agitated or introverted. In some instances, there is the likelihood of developing depression too. The mind engineering wisdom needs to be passed on to young couples and future parents to develop an emotionally mature and competent next generation.

In order to liberate ourselves from the control of the ego-mind and move closer to awakening, it is essential to be aware of various strategies and illusions of the ego-mind. The following are the important illusions and strategies the ego-mind adopts and follows for its survival and strengthening.

ORIGIN, GROWTH AND OPERATION OF THE EGO-MIND

i. We receive information and perceive the world mainly through sensory signals, but the ego-mind misinterprets information received as per its perception to suit its beliefs and image.

ii. The ego-mind has an 'I know' attitude, which creates a closed mind and hinders the flow of new wisdom, such that change is avoided.

iii. The ego-mind treats others as unequal, mainly inferior, so disharmony and conflict will be common.

iv. It has a sense of doubt about new things and experiences, which restricts new wisdom.

v. The ego-mind selectively erases memory or forgets new wisdom received, which are against its beliefs, so that the change is successfully avoided.

vi. The ego-mind believes in the material world and in the past-present-future continuum or linearity.

vii. The ego-mind rigidly identifies with its image.

viii. The ego-mind exists relating to past and future, especially the immediate past and future. Viewing those as real, it justifies the negative emotional reactions to the past and future.

ix. It has rigid expectations every moment that everything should be as per its desires, so that it can create pain and conflict.

x. It resists unfavourable life situations with emotional reactions, and creates conflict and pain.

xi. It does not have an open mind to respect others' points of view, resulting in arguments and conflicts frequently.

xii. The ego-mind has a tendency of being hung up on emotions that have already been experienced.

xiii. It allows the mind to wander while doing nothing, as the wandering mind is negative.

xiv. In order to protect its position, it justifies itself by finding fault with others.
xv. It lacks intimacy with others, which ends up in leading to frequent conflicts.
xvi. The ego-mind always prompts mind chatter or incessant thoughts, so that we are not fully in the present.
xvii. An emotional reaction pattern is followed, attributing reasons to some cause so that negative emotions are justified and the pattern is continued.
xviii. The ego-mind's identification is limited to body and image, and it does not sincerely accept the spiritual aspect and its relevance.

We have received a deeper understanding of the ego-mind and its dynamics, which will help us reduce its strength and control over us and move closer to the state of awakening. In this process, we also need to address the immediate effect of ego-mind's operation on us, i.e., creating an emotional reaction pattern and resultant pain in our lives.

8

FREEDOM FROM EMOTIONAL REACTION AND PAIN

A good percentage of the present generation is living in financial security and experiencing a high 'quality' of life. They have a lifestyle of pleasures and enjoyments. Simultaneously, a large portion of unfortunate people is suffering from financial constraints and related miseries. The purpose of the higher wisdom of soul consciousness and various mind engineering practices is to have a life of peace and joy, which we cannot purchase with wealth. This peace and joy are missing from life, mainly due to our negative emotional reaction patterns or the mental pain we have been harbouring. A clear understanding and higher awareness about it will help us change and achieve this goal in life. When we can free ourselves from the negative emotional reaction pattern, the benefits will be drastic and twofold:

i. We will reduce pain in life and bring happiness, wellness and good health.
ii. We will reduce the strength of the ego-mind and its control on us and gradually break free from its grip, and be able to move towards awakening.

It is a misconception that the so-called elite or wealthy live in happiness; happiness or joy is different from pleasure, which is an elevated feeling derived from controlled situations. Happiness or joy implies a positive and elevated state of mind from within and the absence of pain. If we analyse it in this context, we can see that most people in the economically and socially well-to-do strata are not in a peaceful and joyous state of mind most of the time and live in a state of tension, stress, depression, anger and the list goes on. This means that most of us are in a constant state of conflict and mental pain.

Pain

There are basically two categories of pain—mental pain and physical pain. Here we refer to mental pain, but we will also refer to physical pain as an example to better understand mental pain. All negative emotions, whether mild or severe, from uneasiness to extreme anger, depression, sadness or stress, fall in the category of mental pain. As these emotions are common for everybody in daily life, they are always taken for granted. Hence, Buddha stated that *dukkha* (suffering) is a basic nature of human beings.

Emotion and Health

We know that there are positive and negative emotions. Medical science has shown that positive emotions produce many healthy biochemicals in the body and vice versa. Negative emotions, when experienced for a long duration of time, result in many diseases. For example, stress or threat experience produces stress hormones, such as cortisol, and inflammatory agents, like cytokines, that stop cells from growing and adversely affect the immune system. The emotion of love produces neurochemicals, such as dopamine, oxytocin and growth hormones, which are associated with health and wellness.

When we experience negative emotions, our body turns on its protective mode and directs blood, energy and other resources to face adverse situations. When we are in our natural state of peace and joy, our body is in the growth mode by protecting itself, growing and rejuvenating every second. When there is pain, we cannot focus our energy and efforts rationally on various day-to-day activities of life effectively. Much of our energy gets eroded due to negative emotions, and we are not able to lead a normal life with peace of mind and happiness. Look at children—they are usually healthy, happy and playful, which shows that we are by nature oriented to be healthy and happy. Neuroscientists endorse this view and say that our brains are naturally wired to be happy.[1]

Perception and Pain

Based on the childhood experiences and influence of others' perceptions of us, we have developed a kind of phobia about physical pain, and hence it multiplies the gravity of pain in different situations. For example, many are scared of injections. For them, the magnitude of an injection's pain is much more severe than the reality of the pain, which is negligible. There are people having an extreme phobia about certain harmless insects (entomophobia); on the other hand, certain communities eat such insects happily. Our perception about (mental) pain spoils our valuable life, creates hellish experience in life, destroys relationships, creates conflicts, and, hence, it is something everybody wants to avoid at any cost. Usually, we think that mental pain only refers to sadness, but it is not so. Any negative emotion that results in denial of mental peace and happiness falls under the category of mental pain. In short, all negative feelings and emotions fall under the category of mental pain. It is mostly manifested and experienced in response to unfavourable life situations.

People are willing to spend any amount of time and money to avoid mental pain and have good health and happiness in life. They are aware that the root causes of mental pain are negative thoughts and emotions, and they want to replace them with positive ones. There are many programmes, like meditations, counselling and stress management now. However, we have rarely seen people practise these regularly and meticulously; most of them go back to their old lifestyle due to the ego-mind's resistance. It is possible to sustainably reduce mental pain in life if we are fully aware of its various aspects, change our perception about it at the subconscious mind level and reprogramme our default mode. Let us study it minutely so that we can reduce pain to a great extent and bring happiness and good health in life.

As discussed earlier, we all have developed fear psychosis about physical pain in different degrees. Irrational fear about physical pain is also rooted in identification with body consciousness. It is evident from the fact that different people react differently to similar life situations. Let us slightly modify the earlier example. If three people are given medical injections, one may react with fear very intensively and the other person may take it with a cool mind. The third person, a rare category of spiritually advanced beings, may use it as an opportunity to experience presence with a smiling face. So far, we have been justifying our pains by attributing reasons to some unfavourable life situations because of unconsciousness. From the above example, where three people react differently to the same situation, we become aware that our negative emotional reactions or pains are not due to the life situations but due to our nature or subconscious mind pattern.

Physical Pain: A Gift

Though we have developed a phobia about physical pain, the fact is that physical pain is a great gift of nature. It indicates malfunctions or injuries in the body, so that we can take corrective measures and get back to being healthy. The first and foremost parameter of diagnosis of physical illness is the nature of pain. In the absence of pain, our survival comes under question, and, hence, it is clear that physical pain is a blessing for human beings to survive and remain healthy. It is nature's precious gift. Now lets us come to the crux of the subject, which is mental pain.

Mental Pain

As in the case of physical pain, we have a negative perception of mental pain. In both cases, we wish to avoid it and get to its root cause, if we are afflicted. As there are so many types and categories of mental pain, patterns of reaction and manifestations, for the sake of better understanding and addressing it, we need to narrow it down to negative emotional reactions, which is the most common and critical problem in life for most of us. This higher awareness about mental pain and emotional reaction pattern will help us reprogramme our subconscious mind programme and break free from it, moving closer to the state of awakening.

Negative Emotional Reaction

Negative emotions are a natural part of our life and are required in certain situations. The typical example is of a caveman facing a tiger in the jungle. He must be in a stressful situation and fight or flight mode. The stress hormones help in flow of additional blood and energy to the muscles. It is natural to have stressful situations and emotions in life. Some neuroscientists believe that if stress and emotional reactions exist for a short period, they are not much harmful for the body. The problem arises when we experience negative emotional reactions, like stress, habitually, repetitively and irrationally for a long duration. They, then, become unhealthy and dangerous. But the fact is that in most instances, our emotional reactions are not justified by the circumstances alone but also result from the subconscious mind programme and pattern. So, with higher awareness, we can be free from it and bring happiness, health and wellness in life.

Usually, we tend to stick to the negative emotional charge for hours and days irrationally even after the unfavourable life situation has passed. This is the trick of the ego-mind. It uses our intelligence and justifies the emotional reaction and its 'hangover', creating an illusion that the past trigger is still a reality and existing in the now, which is unconsciousness. Here we need to know the basics of the ego-mind dynamics. We are driven mostly by our ego-mind, the false image, and its basic nature is pain, a sense of separateness and a sense of lack. It needs negative emotions or their variants periodically for its survival. Most of the time, there is a pattern of negative emotions that is repetitive in nature. When we experience similar negative emotions each time, the corresponding brain circuits are strengthened, and the pattern becomes rigid gradually.

Happiness Ratio

The purpose of reducing negative emotions is to bring in more happiness in life. When happiness is the goal of life, we need to know how happy we are every day. We can think in terms of a ratio between the duration of happiness and unhappiness in daily life. We usually never bother to assess it. The ego-mind always wants pain and conflict; it wants to avoid happiness. We can be happy only in the present moment, so the ego-mind's strategy becomes to deny the present moment's experience to us. If we introspect, we realize that we are not fully in the present most of the time. Usually, we consider only severe unhappiness as a problem, and mild forms of unhappiness are considered common and natural. But the fact is that any mild form of unhappiness is also a state of unhappiness. When our goal is to have happiness, our ego-mind's goal and strategy becomes to experience unhappiness or pain. The ego-mind has been successful as our happy time is far less compared to unhappy time. We are not aware of it. Suppose we are unhappy 90 per cent of the time (liberal estimate) and happy 10 per cent of the time; the ego-mind wants to be stronger by gradually increasing the time of unhappiness or pain. We see many people around who gradually become increasingly unhappy in life over a period, despite their good fortune. If you meet a person after a few years, his face will seem to have lost grace and happiness compared to an earlier time. Suppose somebody always wants to see you unhappy and is continuously putting efforts in that direction. What will you call him? Enemy! Yes, the ego-mind is doing the same thing in your life, knowing fully that unhappiness and negative emotions will adversely affect our health and life. Hence the ego-mind is the number one enemy in our life. As most of our unhappiness or pain is experienced through negative emotional reactions, addressing the issue is a matter of urgency.

Usually, the ego-mind will not allow us to reduce pain and enhance our happiness level. The ego-mind has a clear strategy to maintain unhappiness or pain at the present level and gradually increase it over a period of time. We see certain occasions when people experience happiness and joy much more than the usual level on a day. The ego-mind will then find some reason and create situations to create pain and compensate for the happy time.

Deep Dive into Negative Emotional Reactions

Our conscious mind is aware that negative emotional reactions, like anger, create pain, spoil relationships and the charm of our entire lives. Hence, we need to liberate ourselves from it, change or transform with higher awareness by diving deep into it. Though we experience many types of mental pains daily, we can identify the dominant one, which is frequently manifested with severe intensity—anger. Our strategy is to address the dominant emotional pain that is rooted in our subconscious mind, so that mild ones automatically get resolved with our higher awareness and practice. So, our strategy is twofold: one, to address the root cause of the dominant negative emotional reactions with higher awareness, and, two, to address the manifestations of these dominant emotional reactions.

Analysis of Dominant Negative Emotional Reactions

We have seen that physical pain is a blessing and so is mental pain. Mental pain or emotional reaction pattern is a blessing, as it is the window to become aware of the root cause of the dominant emotional reaction. Only with this awareness can we liberate ourselves from it.

For a clearer understanding of mental pain, such as anger, we can refer to physical pain as an example. Imagine that there are many thorns stuck in our leg. They create pain, indicating the presence of thorns, and we usually remove them. But suppose some thorns remain inside without our awareness, and the skin outwardly gets healed. We may experience some pain in daily life, with severe pain each time the thorns' spots are hit. This will frequently happen until we become fully aware of the thorns inside, undergo minor surgery, and fully remove them. This is what is happening in the case of mental pain or anger. There are negative emotional experiences and pain which are stored in the subconscious mind during our childhood without our awareness. When we have similar life situations like those experienced in childhood, it hits or triggers that spot of emotional storage/thorn and creates similar emotions/pain and manifests it. For example, we might have been hurt or angry or experienced others getting angry in certain situations back when we were children—that might have become a part of our subconscious programme. When there is a similar situation, we repeat the same pattern after becoming adults as per the subconscious programme. When we become aware of this truth, its dynamics and bring awareness to the childhood situations in which we experienced the negative emotions and make sense of it (thorns in the mind), it will start getting resolved. As we discussed earlier, the ego-mind wants pains, and hence this is how it creates pain without our awareness. Sometimes, when the ego-mind needs pain, it wrongly interprets some events or life situations and makes us believe that this experience is like the one stored in the subconscious mind and prompts us to create corresponding thoughts, emotions and conflict or pain. Another way the ego-mind repeats the same pattern of creating pain is by having an illusion in the mind, as explained below.

The Illusion of Cause and Effect

Usually, our mind justifies our emotional reactions or nature with a cause and effect approach, i.e., 'My X emotional reaction is because of Y reason; I got angry because of this or that reason.' This justification is the ego-mind's strategy for not realizing the real cause and resisting change. We can see it in how different teachers react differently to the same naughty behaviour of students, which proves that the effect (reaction) is not because of cause (trigger), but because of the person's nature or the subconscious programme.

Narrowing Down to Anger and Its Management

Let us further narrow down the emotional reaction pattern to anger and its solution, as, for most of you, anger is the most severe emotional reaction and a persistent problem in life, both at workplace and home. We all know that emotion is experienced in the mind, and proper awareness is most critical to fix any problem related to the mind. So, let us address the negative emotion of anger closely.

Anger is a negative emotional reaction to an unfavourable or unexpected situation. For better understanding, let us refer to an example of a common situation where we get angry, and become aware of its dynamics. We can consider the example of an angry teacher when he comes across a naughty student. If you ask the teacher about why he is angry, he will say that it is due to the student's naughty behaviour. We all do the same thing in similar situations. We attribute the reason for anger to an unfavourable situation or another person's behaviour. This is fundamentally incorrect. To become aware of this fundamental truth, just think about whether all teachers react with the same degree of anger to the student's naughty behaviour. We know the answer is no. Another teacher may lovingly advise the same naughty student. Different people react differently to the same situation.

What does it mean then? It means that the anger is not due to a situation or incident; it is based on each person's nature or subconscious programme. Some people are aware of their angry nature, but say they cannot control or change it. The conclusion is that a person's anger or negative emotional reaction is not because of a situation or incident but because of his nature. It means that emotional behaviour is as per our subconscious programme, which we are not aware of. This fundamental awareness and repeated introspection on this aspect will help us reprogramme our subconscious mind. This will gradually reduce our anger in general. If a person is aware of the childhood situations and experiences that resulted in the programme, he becomes aware of the cause behind his angry nature. In such cases, the reprogramming or arriving at the solution is much easier. Again, come back to our example. The question is whether the same teacher would be angry in the same manner at the same incident that had happened a month earlier?

No. It is a past event and not a reality anymore. The teacher or any sensible person is also aware that an emotional reaction or anger towards something that has already happened in the past is foolishness because the situation does not exist now. Here is the critical question: is it not a fact that an event that happened one minute earlier is also a 'past event'? This past event is also something unreal and something that does not exist now. This truth is contrary to our belief so far. Whether it is one year before or one month before, or even one minute before, any incident that has happened is the past and is unreal and does not exist now. Therefore, anger towards something that occurred in the past, even a minute earlier, is also unconsciousness or foolishness. In short, our anger or nature of negative emotional reactions is nothing but unconsciousness or foolishness. We know that the ego-mind wants emotional conflict and pain for its survival. The ego-mind creates the illusion that the immediate past and future are a reality and exist in the present, so that conflict and pain are created and justified for the survival of the ego-mind. It does not mean that we should accept all situations; we can rationally respond to them as needed.

When a person becomes fully aware of this truth and lives a life of being 100 per cent present, there is no room for emotional reaction or anger. In the present, the ego-mind does not control us, and only true self and rationality drive us. Our brain circuits are structured and strengthened as per the experiences and patterns of thoughts and emotions. The ability of our brain to structure itself as per experiences is called neuroplasticity, so the brain tends to continue to have similar thoughts and emotional patterns. It needs deeper introspection, awareness, new experiences and meditation to change the brain circuits, so that we can break the pattern and the tendency to repeat it and sustainably transform ourselves.

From the above explanation, we are now aware that when we are angry frequently, the 'anger-thorn' is the dominant wound inside, and we should become aware of how it came to exist and how it is triggered, causing pain or anger. This awareness will gradually reduce the pattern, and we will be eventually entirely free from anger. Similarly, we can address other emotional reactions and take out other 'thorns' and permanently heal the wounds.

When our subconscious mind drives us, its nature is manifested in life situations by generating negative emotions, like fear, anger, sadness, depression, hurt, rage, dread, etc., and, in the long run, it affects our health and wellness. As we live in an unconscious state, unaware of the subconscious mind, we do not know the real reasons behind our negative emotions and the ways and means for having and experiencing healthy and positive emotions, like love and joy. The root causes of our negative emotions are the behavioural pattern based on our subconscious mind programme of which we are not aware and our emotional reactions believing that the past and future are real and existing. We know that emotionally reacting to something unreal is not sanity. As we believe the past and future to be real, which is an illusion and not existing, we react to it emotionally, relating to the past worries and anxieties of the future. So negative emotional reactions are there only when we believe in the illusion that the past and future are real. In the absence of it, rational responses and natural positive emotions will start emerging and manifesting automatically. To bring it into the realistic realm, we need to become fully aware of the unconsciousness or illusions we have been carrying. Now we are aware that the past-present-future continuum is an illusion, and the present moment is the reality, and it exists in isolation, which we can experience. We have to bring in higher awareness, like shedding light in a dark area, and realize that the present moment is the only reality in which we can live and experience everything. We should start segregating the present from the past and future or linear experience of the world by experiencing the present moment and rationally responding to each moment or present life situation.

Now we are in a state of higher awareness about our ego-mind and those of others too. With the strength of this wisdom, we are going to gain further higher wisdom, which is very subtle, and will require close attention and an open mind. This will help us break free from a lot of mental pain and suffering.

Why Emotional Reaction Instead of a Rational Response?

Our brainstem is involved in sudden reflex reactions when there is a threat, and our emotional or limbic brain is active when we emotionally react based on our subconscious programme, which is on 'autopilot'. Studies show that it takes less than a second to trigger an emotional reaction.[2] The most frequent situation creating severe emotional pain is unfavourable life situations involving people's interactions. Such life situations are more complex and dynamic when they involve more than one ego-mind and its conflicts. Higher awareness of this truth at a deeper and experiential level will help us make a huge difference to our life by eliminating conflicts and pain from such life situations, bringing in more joy. Let us understand this truth in detail.

The Practical Dimension of Emotional Reactions

The ego-mind justifies all emotional reactions saying that they are being caused by an unfavourable situation or a particular trigger, so that it can continue this practice and pattern the whole life, creating conflict and pain. If we observe people reacting emotionally, we can see that it has a pattern, periodicity and nature because it arises from the compulsiveness of the subconscious mind. We can also observe that emotional reactions are much more intensive than the required response to a situation or a trigger. Sometimes a serious look or assertive statement is only necessary for unacceptable behaviour of another person, but many people react severely due to the replay of childhood experiences or subconscious programmes. A higher awareness and close self-observation will help us break free from these compulsive patterns. For example, a person who was compelled to do strenuous physical labour in childhood may emotionally react severely if someone asks him to do some minor physical work when he grows up. A person who felt abandoned in childhood may feel extremely bad emotionally and react abnormally for frivolous reasons to situations like a taxi coming late, spouse getting late in picking them up or somebody not responding to their telephone call, etc.

We need to understand emotional reactions with a deeper awareness. We have different types of life situations with and without interaction with others. Consider a life situation without human interaction as an example. Suppose we are walking in the hot sun and get angry as an emotional reaction to heat. Is it wise and rational? We know it is not wise, and rather foolish. It is foolishness because emotional reaction to reality is foolishness, it will do no good and only aggravate the situation.

What would be a rational approach?

i. If walking in the sun can be avoided, avoid it.
ii. If it cannot be avoided, modify the situation to suit yourself. Try using a shade or an umbrella.
iii. If modifying the situation is also not possible, accept it as a reality. Feel the sun dispassionately to deepen the experience of presence, and decide to face it rationally. This will give you mental strength and minimize the impact of the situation on your body and mind.

Such a rational approach to every unfavourable life situation without human interaction will help us face it rationally, effectively and evolve spiritually.

Life Situations with Human Interactions

Now let us see the life situations with human interactions and emotional reactions. This is the most critical aspect that frequents in our daily lives, either in family, workplace or society. We have seen that the negative emotional reaction pattern creates a lot of severe problems in all spheres of life.

As the reactionary pattern is deep-rooted beyond our conscious mind's primary consciousness level, we need to 'dissect' it carefully for clear and full awareness. For example, do we get hurt if a child aged three uses an offensive word prompted by another person? No, because we know that the child is unaware of its meaning and relevance. Suppose a mentally unstable person uses such words; most of us will not mind it; we would think rationally that he is mentally unstable and unaware. If a security man in the street shouts an offensive word at a bystander near you, you may not like it, but would not get hurt. If it is towards you, it will hurt, and you will react emotionally, with or without manifestation. When it is in the presence of your friends, the gravity of the hurt magnifies. From the above examples, we can draw certain conclusions.

We react with negative emotions only if it comes from a person who is fully aware of the trigger and intended to emotionally hurt us or our ego-mind. And its impact is magnified when it is noticed by others, especially those known to us. Our reaction is not to a situation, but is based on the state of mind of others. This is an awareness of a higher order. With higher awareness about the ego-mind and its dynamics, we become aware that emotional reactions of others towards us arise from a state of subconscious program, like in the case of a child or a mentally unstable person in the street. Hence, there is an important point to be aware of: with the unconsciousness created by our ego-mind, we have been reacting not to the people but to their provocations or unconsciousness. We do not judge and emotionally react to a child based on his emotional behaviour; in the case of adults, we judge them based on their emotional behaviour or egoic behaviour, and emotionally react to them. This is unconsciousness or irrational behaviour on our part. Our emotional reaction to another ego-mind is also irrational or foolish on our part, and we should respond to it with rationality, love and compassion. If we react emotionally to others' ego-mind provocations, it is as good as emotionally reacting to a child or a mentally unstable person. Now, we can distinguish between a person and his ego-mind patterns. We should not emotionally react to another ego-mind but rationally respond to the person or situation, just like we do while interacting with children.

Our quality of life depends on the quality of our state of mind when we are conscious, our quality of thoughts, emotions and feelings. Deep and higher awareness about the ego-mind dynamics will help us become aware of all the strategies and operations of the subconscious program and the ego-mind. We will then be able to experience a paradigm shift in the way we deal with life situations, i.e., from emotional reaction pattern to rational response pattern.

The difference between the rational response and emotional reaction is that the latter is towards a person or a situation when triggered by the subconscious mind programme without our awareness; the rational response is towards the person or situation, as per the situation's need. While an angry teacher would get angry with all students even for their minor mistakes (emotional reaction), an awakened teacher's response would be in tandem with the requirement of the situation. A serious look, a warning or a loving advice might suffice for the latter (rational reaction).

Now we are inching closer to the core of the secret truth about the ego-mind activity regarding emotional reactions or pain. It needs closer attention, understanding and deeper awareness to unravel it and make sense of the strategy of the ego-mind, so that we will be free from the vicious circle of emotional reactions and pain in future. The ego-mind needs to create negative emotions frequently. If we observe people who are immensely controlled by their ego-mind, we can see a pattern and periodicity in their emotional conflicts. If such emotions or pain could not be created in the usual periodicity due to a change in life situations or any other reason, the ego-mind will feel that something is amiss and build up irritation or unease for want of such emotion or pain. If such a situation is not available, the ego-mind will initiate action or inaction to provoke other's ego-mind and create conflict and pain. In the absence of a life situation for an emotional conflict, the ego-mind may imagine past conflict situations and create pain to feed itself.

People, who are not aware of the ego-mind's dynamics and its compulsive tendencies for conflict and pain, fall prey to the strategy of the ego-mind of other people and get provoked and emotionally react, leading to conflict and pain. This may result in chain reactions, creating severe conflicts and pain.

There is another subtle way in which we can manage ego-mind manifestations and reactions of others based on the higher mind engineering wisdom and awareness of the ego-mind dynamics. When a child is born, he is angelically innocent, and we are aware that the ego-mind or subconscious programme is formed from childhood experiences. It means that we cannot blame a child; the caregivers during a child's initial years and their own life situations play significant roles in developing this programme and its manifestations like emotional reactions. We are now fully aware that it is irrational for us to react to them emotionally. We should keep in mind that emotional reactions are manifestations of the subconscious programme, which is formed during childhood. Thus, these are essentially a 'child's expression in an 'adult' manner—through way of words, tone, body language etc. A rational person has love and compassion for a child who reacts emotionally; similarly, we should have love and compassion while responding to the ego-mind's manifestations among others, as these are unconscious expressions of the 'child' within them. This higher awareness will also help us respond rationally and avoid conflicts in life. This does not mean that we should accept all situations and behaviour of others. We can assertively respond to such situations when required, and that will be more effective than emotional reactions.

Now we are fully aware of important aspects emotional pain created by the ego-mind and its practical dimensions, which are summarized as under:

i. **Higher awareness about emotional reaction and rational response:** As managing emotional pain through a rational response is a critical aspect of our life, we need to have in-depth awareness about it. When we are emotionally reacting, we are driven by our ego-mind. With higher awareness and mind engineering wisdom, we become aware of the ego-mind's pattern and are able to gradually shift to the pattern of rational response to life situations.

ii. **Who perceives the situation?** We have to be aware of who is perceiving a situation involving the ego-mind of another person: us or our ego-mind. For example, a colleague is talking to you in anger. If your ego-mind is perceiving it, your emotional reaction pattern will be activated, and you will either react emotionally with anger or feel hurt or sad, which will create a chain of emotional reactions and conflicts. With higher awareness of ego-mind dynamics, you can be aware of the emotional reactions triggered by the subconscious programmes of others, in this case, the colleague's anger. If your true self, and not the ego-mind, is perceiving and responding to emotional reactions of others, the anger of other people, you will respond rationally. The awareness of and ability to distinguish between the person and their ego-mind will help us respond rationally to other people and avoid conflict and pain in life.

iii. **What do you pay attention to?** When we emotionally react to other people' emotions, we give attention to the other person's ego-mind and not to the entire situation or the person. If a child is crying, we will not emotionally react with anger or sadness; we pay attention to the child as a whole and rationally respond to the situation; we do not react emotionally. This wisdom should apply when we interact with the ego-minds or emotions of other people. If a psychiatrist is interacting with a patient who is violent or uttering unpleasant words, he will not emotionally react to what the patient did or said, but will assess the situation of the patient and rationally react to it. He will do what is required for the patient. But when it comes to the people's emotional action/reaction, our ego-mind, as a strategy, does not allow us to respond rationally to the situation; instead, our emotional reaction patterns are triggered and expressed to the other's ego-mind. We should be aware of the situation and person as a whole instead of sticking to ego-mind's provocation of others, and rationally respond to the situation.

Managing Emotional Pain

We have seen that ego-mind has an addictive and compulsive tendency to create pain. With mind engineering wisdom, we are now aware of these ego-mind dynamics. Let us see an example for further clarity. For example, one person frequently gets hurt by others. With higher awareness and close introspection, he identifies the nature of the emotional pain and hurt he has been experiencing; though the conscious mind wants to avoid hurtful situations in life, it still happens frequently. This is because, as we have seen, the ego-mind wants the same negative emotions as it experienced in the past to feed and strengthen itself. It attracts what is inside us; 'like attracts like'—law of attraction. Without this awareness, the person keeps suffering all through his life, creating pain.

Being fully aware of the dynamics of pain, we achieve a state of insight, i.e., we become aware of what and why we think, feel and behave in a particular manner. With this insight, we should closely observe the thoughts, emotions and behavioural patterns the ego-mind is creating. Initially, we may be aware of this strategy of the ego-mind after the occurrence of the situation. Gradually, we will be able to identify and observe it when there would be thoughts and tendencies or an urge to create such situations. Later on, we will break free from such strategies.

Our ego-mind creates a lot of emotional pain in our life by unnecessarily bothering about 'what others think' and struggling to get the appreciation and attention of others. This aspect of ego-mind has developed as a 'syndrome' that needs a detailed examination and in-depth awareness.

'What Others Think' Syndrome

This is the basis of maximum conflicts and pain in the world of the ego-mind. In the ancient world, people were predominantly body-conscious; in the face of a conflict, they fought each other to physically harm or overpower their enemy. In today's modern world, we are ego-conscious, and we identify with our ego-mind image. So during conflict with an enemy, the aim becomes to cause damage to their ego-mind image. The impact of the attack will depend upon the gravity of 'what others think'. We have also seen that the ego-mind emotionally reacts to the ego-minds of others, not to the person. The ego-mind harbours negative thoughts and emotions most of the time, and our ego-mind expects that others should not think negatively about us. This expectation has no rational basis as we cannot control the thoughts and emotions of others. Everyone is thinking, feeling and behaving as per their ego-mind. Usually, we feel pain when others or our adversaries are trying to harm our ego-mind image. So, if we feel pain when our adversaries attack our image (ego-mind), it means we still identify with our ego-mind image.

We have seen, as a victim, how we create pain for ourselves; if our ego-mind is strong, we become perpetrators, create conflict and pain for ourselves and others. In both scenarios, the critical point is that our ego-mind state depends on 'what others think', which means that others control our thoughts, emotions and actions. We should break free from this illusion of being happy, depending on others' thoughts and feelings. We should have this higher awareness that we cannot control others' thoughts; whatever others think and feel is in accordance with their subconscious program or nature. What you expect does not make any difference to the thought patterns of others. We should know that regardless of our expectations or us feeling bothered, people with negative minds will continue thinking negatively and those with positive minds will go on thinking positively about us, come what may. Then why do we worry about what others think? We should be bothered about what we think and feel, as our quality of life depends on it. For that purpose, we should have a higher awareness about what our minds usually do, how the ego-mind operates to deny us the present moment and happiness.

'What others think' syndrome becomes severe when we are faced with a life situation that are damaging our image. Because of the mind engineering wisdom, we are now aware that unfavourable situations in life are not a problem but a reality, and all we can do is face them rationally. This approach will help us gain strength and face those situations. When we are aware that we should live in the reality, i.e., present, it will bring us strength, rationality and the ability to face the situations, while being rooted in the present. We are aware that we cannot control what others think. We need to shift our attention from what others think to what we think and feel. We need not bother about what others think and worry unnecessarily, but we need to be concerned about our precious lives, minds, thoughts and feelings.

When we say that we should only bother about what we think and feel, it does not mean that we are insensitive to what others think and feel, or we do not need approval, goodwill and recognition of others. We all feel good when we are recognized by others; it is natural, and there is nothing wrong with it. What we are talking about is the rigid craving of the subconscious programme for others' acceptance of our ego-created image and the emotional pain we experience when others think against our expectations, needs and image of the ego-mind. This higher awareness about the ego-mind pattern will help us break free from a lot of pain and brings in more happiness and awakening in life.

9

THOUGHTS AND ENERGY

We have moved ahead in our spiritual journey towards awakening; we have addressed resistance of our ego-mind to change, the question of who we are, the ego-mind dynamics and the subtle aspects of emotional pain. Now we are addressing subtler aspects, like thoughts and energy, which are the fundamental aspects of human experiences. Everything is energy at the deepest level of our existence, and so are our thoughts. Deep awareness about thoughts and energy will help us change our certain basic perceptions and beliefs, which will help us make a shift in awareness from our materialist perceptions or unconscious state to higher awareness about the self, others and the world around, and move further towards awakening.

An awakened state implies a state of mind with positive thoughts and a higher level of mental energy. As the mind engineering process of transformation is based on higher awareness, full focus of attention and deeper experience of now, we need to have a basic awareness of body/brain and mind functions, especially thoughts and energy, which are fundamental to human existence. The transformation or awakening process involves a shift in awareness; this shift transforms the nature of a person's thoughts and energy, which are the fundamental aspects of human beings. We have seen the relevance and importance of thoughts in life in earlier chapters.

Thoughts

We have about 60,000–70,000 thoughts in a day.[1] Out of this range, about 70 per cent are negative,[2] and about 90 per cent are same as the day before.[3] Thoughts are very powerful; stress can be produced by thoughts alone. Our energy level also depends on the nature of the thoughts we generate. In short, our life, more specifically the quality of our life, depends on the nature of our thoughts. The nature of our thoughts decides the nature of our personality, physiology, biochemistry, wellness, mental state, illnesses, healing, higher experiences and energy level—in short, quality of our life. Norman Vincent Peale popularized the impacts of positive and negative thinking among people, especially among medical professionals.[4]

As most of the genes are expressed based on our thoughts, and as most of our thoughts are negative and the same every day, we create the same experiences and the same biochemistry every day. Majority of the genes (estimated range from 75–85 per cent) are turned off and on by signals from our environment, including the thoughts, beliefs and emotions that we cultivate in our brains.[5] Depending on the nature of thoughts, chemical signals are sent to the cells' nucleus, corresponding DNAs are triggered and proteins are produced in the cells for various physical needs. It implies that if we want to change our body, heal or have a new life, the secret lies in the type of thoughts we have and their patterns. The most important thing that we should learn and teach others, especially the younger generation, is the importance of thoughts.

The brain has a complex network of nerve cells, neurons, all interacting together and creating an electric field. Wherever there is a nerve cell, there is an electric activity. All forms of energy, like light and sound, are present in the form of waves.

Since these are electric waves, our thoughts are governed by the standard rules of energy in quantum mechanics. So our thoughts are formed in the electrical field, which is measurable; common medical equipment can measure all electrical impulses of our bodies. In short, thoughts are nothing but energy. The type, nature and strength of thoughts depend on each thought wave's frequency and force. Each thought wave is a distinct form of quality and force. When a positive thought is disseminated into the universe with great force, it spreads in space and strikes the minds of people having a similar wavelength or like-mindedness or resonance; those who receive such thoughts, and in turn think positive things of similar frequency charge the universe with similar positive thoughts. Studies have shown that DNA molecules can be altered with intention when we are in a state of heart coherence.[6]

We are transceivers; we transmit and receive thoughts. We transmit thoughts depending on the nature of our perceptions and beliefs; their frequency and wavelength depend on the nature of these thoughts. As most of our thoughts are negative, we mostly send out negative thoughts, and, like mobile connections, we also have a list of contacts/people in our network. Primarily, our signals reach all those who are in our network. All may not notice the message or signal and respond to it; only those who resonate with our message react to it in different ways as per their nature. A massive study involving 689,003 Facebook users found that emotional contagion does not require direct contact between people.[7] The study reports, 'Emotion expressed by others on Facebook influence our own emotion, constituting experimental evidence for massive-scale contagion via social networks.' Similarly, our thoughts trigger the minds of those with similar mindsets or resonance, and pop up and generate corresponding thoughts, emotions and actions in them. So, positive or negative emotion is a contagion.[8] At the secondary level, these thought waves sent out will influence other people who have similar resonance and trigger their corresponding thoughts and consequential actions. A large study involving 11,739 people for 20 years showed how our thoughts and emotions affect others.[9] When we interact with a happy and positive person, we can boost our positivity for a period of up to one year; one's positive and happy state of mind affects others around them. This also shows that we are all connected and exist within a larger field of consciousness. Many of us have experienced instances of receiving phone calls from close people the moment we think about them, or they say our phone call was received the moment they thought about us. Thoughts or messages provoking thoughts, among others, are manifested more in the case of negative thoughts that are processed in the strong left hemisphere of the brain.

One typical example is the gruesome rape incident that happened in Delhi in 2012. The incident was widely condemned and a lot of protests were organized intending to prevent such incidents in the future, which pushed the law-enforcement machinery to take stringent actions. Everybody thought that there would be a drastic reduction of such incidents in the future. But astonishing everyone, police records show that rape incidents almost doubled in Delhi next year.[10] The widespread newscasts and discussions on rape triggered related thoughts in people's minds who had tendencies to become perpetrators of such crimes. Similarly, positive thoughts also trigger other minds positively. A study conducted by Duke University involving 866 heart patients reported that patients with positive emotions lived 11 years more than those with habitual negative emotions.[11]

Negative Thoughts

Negative thoughts have a direct impact on health. It was found that people with a hostile attitude had five times more chance of having coronary heart disease.[12] The life of every human being involves interaction with others, and, most of the time, it is not cordial due to arguments, difference of opinions, conflicting views, preferences, attitude, interests, perceptions, beliefs, lifestyle, etc. That ends up becoming the source of most of our sufferings. In addition to manifested conflicts, there are many unmanifested conflicts at the level of thoughts and mild negative emotions within us, which are also equally harmful in life. Negative thoughts and emotions or ill will against others harm us in many ways.

i. The negative pattern of thoughts and emotions strengthens the corresponding brain circuits and develops a tendency to repeat the same pattern, making it more difficult to change.

ii. Every negative thought and emotion produces harmful biochemical substances in the body, and, in the long run, it becomes the cause of various illnesses and spoils our health and wellness.

iii. It spoils our relationships with others when we create situations of ill will and conflict.

iv. Science has shown that human beings are transmitters and receivers of thoughts. When we harbour negative thoughts and emotions about others, such thoughts are sent out as electromagnetic waves and received by like-minded people or those with similar resonance, and trigger a chain of similar thoughts, emotions and actions in them. This transceiving takes place with the help of receptors in brain cells. Such negative thoughts ultimately create negative environment for all. To put it in an example, our thoughts are like a ball bouncing back after being thrown at a wall; once we throw it, it will bounce back to us the way it was thrown.

We have seen movies in which villains and heroes have been fighting for a long time. They eventually become aware that they are real brothers, who were separated in childhood, and then embrace each other—this results in a paradigm shift in their awareness, experience and transformation. So the solution to all sufferings is to become aware of higher wisdom at the experiential level that we all are pure living consciousness and part of the larger consciousness.

Thoughts and Brain

The brain creates new connections and circuits depending upon the nature of new thoughts and experiences. When we change our thought pattern, many neurons fire together to support it and create new experiences. New chemicals are produced in neurons, expressing genes for new protein production, leading to the creation of new branches or synapses between neurons. When we repeat a new thought pattern, these connections become stronger, and new circuits and structures are formed. Nobel laureate Eric Kandel said that when a new memory is created based on new thoughts, it stimulates 2,600 new synapses, doubles the number of repetitive thoughts and rewrites subconscious and genetic patterns.[13] This awareness is essential when we decide to reprogramme our subconscious mind pattern for transformation and awakening. It is required to reinforce mind engineering wisdom and the experience of new positive emotions and practise them daily, including meditation, to make a robust neurological structure and make changes sustainable and permanent.

When a lot of neurons fire in unison to support a new thought, an additional chemical (a protein) is created within the nerve cell and makes its way to the cell's control center, or nucleus, where it lands in the DNA. The protein then switches on several genes. Since the genes' job is to make proteins that maintain both the structure and function of the body, the nerve cell then quickly makes new proteins to create new branches between nerve cells. So when we repeat a thought or an experience many times, our brain cells make not only stronger connections between each other (which affects our physiological functions) but also a greater number of total connections (which affects the physical structure of the body). The brain becomes more enriched microscopically. Neurons 'fired together are wired together'.

Importance of Thoughts

Every thought is an electromagnetic wave sent out to the universe or to the 'field'. Thoughts are very powerful and manifest in the form of words, ideas or messages, and later become emotions and actions. Actions become habits, habits become character, and our character finally influences our destiny. Mahatma Gandhi said, '[...]What he thinks, he becomes[...]' Modern science also tells the same thing, and in the recent past, many scientists said that the mind becomes the body, and so the mind and the body are inseparable entities, and they use one word, which is 'bodymind.'[14] Science has taught us that positive thoughts produce positive chemical substances that are good for health, and negative thoughts produce harmful chemical substances that adversely impact mental and physical health. A Mayo Clinic study from 2002 found that optimists remain healthier physically and mentally.[15] Optimists were also found to live longer compared to non-optimists.[16]

When the atmosphere is charged with good thoughts, good things happen in society. This rule also applies in the case of negative thoughts; when negative thoughts are disseminated in space, it triggers similar thoughts, feelings and actions in people having corresponding frequencies of thoughts or resonance.

Similarly, thought-related processes happen within the brain in different frequencies, and thoughts travel outside the brain in the atmosphere. The brain communicates through neurons, which create electrical potentials that fire and propagate throughout the brain. The pattern of firing is described as brain waves, which are neural oscillations, and are transmitted through brain cells.

You can create different thoughts in the same situation—like, negative and weak or positive and strong. But due to the compulsiveness of the subconscious programmes, we usually create similar negative thoughts most of the time.

Types of Brain Waves

Depending on the nature and quality of thoughts in our brain, it produces different types of brain waves, which can be measured with the help of EEG. The different categories of brain waves are as follows:

Brain Waves Graph

i.

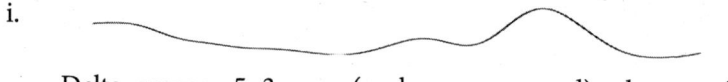

Delta waves, 5–3 cps (cycles per second); deep and dreamless

ii.

Theta waves, 4–7 cps; deeply relaxed or shadow sleep

iii.

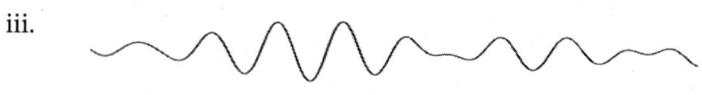

Alpha waves, 8–12 cps; very relaxed meditative state

iv.

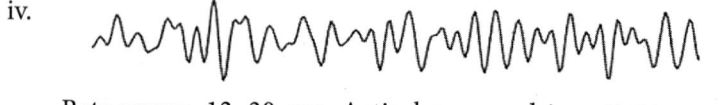

Beta waves, 13–30 cps; Actively engaged in activities and conversation with stress

v.

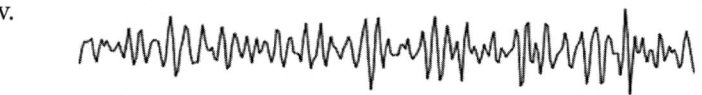

Gamma waves, 31–120 cps; hyper brain activity with deep attention and awareness

Source: Church, Dawson, *Mind to Matter: The Astonishing Science of How Your Brain Creates Material Reality,* Hay House, 2018, pp. 70-2.

Without our awareness, our subconscious mind has a pattern of thoughts and emotions that manifest in our life most of the time. Our life situations and experiences are the results of our thoughts and emotions. As the subconscious mind is driving our majority of thoughts, awareness of this fact will help us reprogramme our subconscious mind, facilitating changes in the pattern of thoughts and bringing transformation in our life.

A wandering mind is a negative mind with many negative thoughts, which involves nurturing, strengthening and reinforcing our ego-mind or false image. Brain areas, like the middle prefrontal cortex (MPFC) and the post cingulate cortex (PCC), are fully active when the mind is wandering. Meditation has the opposite effect and is best for brain relaxation. When a person meditates after a period of mind wandering, it is found that the neural circuits in the PFC are rested and strengthened. This strengthening of neural circuits will help people reduce the mind wandering tendency.

Human Energy

The energy level of a person has a lot of impact on his health and wellness. We need to have certain basic awareness about the various aspects of human energy.

The brain has only 2 per cent of the total body weight, but consumes 20 per cent of resting metabolic rate (RMR) or energy.[17] The average RMR is 1,300 kilocalories (kcal) per day. This means the body needs 54 kcal of energy per hour for its normal functioning, which means 0.9 kcal per minute and 0.15 kcal (15 calories) per second. Fifteen calories approximately equals to 60 watts. This calculation implies that the whole complex body with 40 trillion cells requires energy equal to a 60-watt bulb for its usual functioning, which is inconceivable to common sense.

The Complexity of the Body and Mind Functions

It is estimated that there are about 40 trillion cells in the human body, and each cell performs all bodily functions. So all cells are like a conglomerate of organisms living in harmony. Each cell needs energy to carry out various functions in every moment. The DNA zipper in each cell contains a nucleic acid, called base pairs, numbering at about three billion per cell. Another complicated process happening is cell division; every second, about 810,000 lakh new cells are created in the body.[18] There are approximately 100 billion brain cells or neurons in the brain, with each having about 10,000 synaptic connections. The total number is inconceivable to the human mind; some scientists say that the number is comparable to the total number of subatomic particles in the universe. The human body's important systems that regulate many vital body functions include the integumentary system, skeletal system, muscular system, nervous system, endocrine system, cardiovascular system, respiratory system, digestive system, urinary system and reproductive system.

The generation of each thought involves the firing of a lot of neurons, which also needs energy. The extent of energy consumption of thoughts depends on the nature of thoughts. When a particular brain area is activated with stressful thoughts, more blood and sugar are required for that specific brain area. The brainstem regulates essential body functions and survival circuits, like fight or flight actions, which need a lot of energy and blood supply. The brainstem's thoughts, having high-frequency, require more energy, and, therefore, people who face life-threatening situations cannot continue existing in that state for a long time because they get exhausted fast. Similarly, when negative thoughts are generated, coupled with negative emotions, the limbic brain is activated significantly in the left hemisphere involving a large number of neurons, circuits and synapses that consume a large amount of energy. This is the reason why people are quickly fatigued when feeling emotionally charged or facing stress. On the other hand, when we are engaged in activities with a rational approach, mainly the neocortex is activated for thought, emotions or actions; this part of the brain with a high wavelength and low frequency consumes less energy, and a person can function with a higher energy level and enthusiasm for long hours without fatigue or without adversely affecting his health. This is visible from the activities and lifestyles of spiritually evolved or emotionally mature people. From the above cursory view of the complexity of bodily functions, it is incomprehensible that all bodily functions are taking place with energy equivalent to a 60-watt bulb!

Wellness and health are related to the mental energy level and not the calorie level in the body. In order to feel healthy enough, we need to have a free flow of mental energy in the entire body, without blocks or obstructions. Our nature of thoughts, emotions and lifestyles may create obstructions in the flow of energy. For example, if you are used to sitting in an improper posture for long hours for work in stressed conditions, it is likely to lead to many health issues in the long run, like stiff muscles, neck or joint pains due to obstructions in the free flow of energy in the body. The mental energy level is directly related to our state of mind, and not calorie level or physical strength; our state of mind depends on the nature of thoughts and consequent emotions. For example, a student may be in a state of anxiety and have a low energy level before the announcement of exam results; he may be depressed when the result is far below his expectations. The same student may be full of energy when he comes to know that the announced result was a typing error, and the actual scores are better than what was expected. We have heard that some people exhibit an unimaginable level of physical strength in certain challenging situations. So what is the source of mental energy? Basically, it is our state of mind. This fact explains that people involved in specific tasks that require a higher level of mental energy for success, like sports, can boost their energy level and see better if their mind is engineered properly.

Emerging Aspect of Energy

At the primary consciousness level, we perceive everything in the physical world through sensory perceptions, which is the material dimension. Now, based on quantum mechanics, we are aware that the perception of the solidity or materiality of things is not reality; everything is non-material energy, which has spiritual dimension. A human being is also a dense form of energy with consciousness as its driving force, which is part of a larger consciousness, the field of infinite potential, energy and information, and is in constant mutual interactions with the consciousness of others.

When we consider that billions of complex bodily functions happen every second with the equivalent energy of a 60-watt bulb, it leads us to think that the bodily energy in calories and subtle mental energy are different. The aspect of mental energy or life force of human beings needs greater insight. It gives more credibility to ancient spiritual wisdom that *chi* or *prana* is the life force that drives and coordinates all the body functions, even at the cellular level. This force exists within a larger energy field or cosmic consciousness with continuous mutual interaction, interchange and communication. Here, the words of Nikola Tesla are relevant, 'If you want to find the levels of the universe think in terms of energy, frequency and vibration.'

Energy and Health

Our sensory receptors are capable of detecting and receiving information or signals from the energy field in which we live.[19] Our energy level is very critical for our health and well-being. Occasionally, apart from physiological reasons, we suffer from low energy levels or fatigue because of the adverse life situations and state of mind, coupled with negative thoughts and emotions. We usually overcome such situations within a short duration of time.

Our cells in the body get energy from mitochondria, which are tiny structures that fuel the cells by producing adenosine triphosphate (ATP). If your body has a low energy level, it means that there is a problem in production of enough ATP and, therefore, the cells are drained of energy. Short-term fatigue or less energy is common, which is usually related to negative thoughts and emotions, but long-term sustained fatigue or a lack of energy, even after sufficient intake of calories, is to be taken seriously, as it could be indications of some illnesses. Mental illnesses like depression or anxiety disorders may result in sustained fatigue or energy loss. A better energy level is linked to positive health indicators. Our immune system is directly linked to the energy level of our body. Our body can have a higher energy level if we correctly follow a positive mindset, diet, exercise and sleep routine. But the most important factor is our state of mind, the way we think, feel and behave.

Moderate exercise also boosts the body's energy level, as it promotes neurotransmitters that are involved in promoting energy, such as dopamine, serotonin, norepinephrine, etc. The stress hormone, cortisol, produced by the adrenal gland, reduces ATP production and increases inflammation, which reduces energy levels in the body. Yoga, meditation, mindfulness programmes, etc., can help improve our energy level, health and wellness in life. The energy level is critical, as it affects all aspects of a person's life, including efficiency in personal, social and formal life situations—the quality of life as a whole. Good quality of personal and healthy social relationships is essential for a person to remain mentally elevated and energized. Similarly, strained relationships will create low moods, depressive tendencies and energy loss, adversely affecting all aspects of life.

Relevance of Pranayama

In the yogic tradition, what we breathe is not just oxygen but the life energy, *prana*. The breathing process itself is a spiritual practice, if we observe it closely. Breathing pattern is an indicator of health itself; natural deep breath is an indicator of good health, and short breathing is an indicator of many illnesses or serious health conditions. Less number of breaths in a minute means a deep breath, and the number of deep breaths is related to one's health and lifespan. By doing systematic pranayama or breathing exercises, we can substantially enhance lung capacity and practise deeper breathing, directly impacting health and wellness. We can understand this by looking at the breath duration and lifespan (approximate) of different creatures.

Correlation between Breath Duration and Lifespan

Species	*Breaths-per-minute (Average)*	*Lifespan (Average)*
Mouse	150 BPM	2 years
Rabbit	60 BPM	6 years
Monkey	30 BPM	20 years

Dog	50 BPM	15 years
Human	15-30 BPM	60-80 years
Horse	10-15 BPM	50 years
Whale	4-6 BPM	100 years
Elephant	4-5 BPM	120 years

Yoga and pranayama are much more than mere body or breathing exercises. They also facilitate the use of physique and prana as separate portals to weaken the rigid ego-mind patterns and brain circuits, and move closer to awakening and experiencing consciousness.

Food and Health

Many thoughts and emotions from our childhood become irrelevant when we grow up, and nature envisages that human beings evolve spiritually along with physical growth and development. Most of the problems of grown-ups are due to the absence of corresponding changes in the thoughts, emotions and life pattern envisaged by nature. The feeling of hunger and food habits is a typical example. As far as children are concerned, they are entirely dependent on their caregivers/parents for their survival. They are able to express their needs and emotions when they are hungry, as it is related to survival. But unfortunately, most people carry on the same emotions in the case of food and express it in a similar way when they are hungry, even when they grow up. A mild feeling of hunger per se is not an intolerable severe feeling like other physical or mental pain. However, there are instances when people manifest intense negative emotions while feeling mildly hungry due to the trigger of the subconscious programme.

All health wisdom says that adults should regulate the quantity of food intake and they do not require three or four full meals a day. Many experts say that adults need only one full meal in a day, or if the quantity is reduced, it can be taken two or three times. Intermittent fasting has become the new trend in maintaining good health—Dr Yoshinori Ohsumi got a Nobel Prize in 2016 for this finding. People suffering from health issues, like diabetes, should consult their doctors before considering intermittent fasting. Dr David Sinclair of Harvard University, who leads large research on aging, endorses the same view.[20]

With the above awareness, we can observe and experience the sensation and feeling of mild hunger as a means for enhancing presence without judgement and emotional reaction, and feel a subtle energy within us. This practice can help us regulate our food habits, which can be a higher spiritual practice and a means for good health and wellness. The above higher awareness of thoughts and energy will shed many illusions and wrong perceptions and help us reprogramme our old patterns and automatically move closer to the state of awakening.

Not only do we need a higher level of psychic energy for our good health and wellness, the free flow of energy in the body is also essential. That is why we feel more energetic when doing yoga or moderate whole-body exercises that ensure a seamless flow of energy. On the contrary, if the free flow is obstructed, it will harm your body, and, in the long run, it may manifest as illnesses. When we remain in an unhealthy or unnatural physical posture for a long time, it may obstruct energy flow and create many physical discomforts and problems. People who need to sit for long durations are advised to go on short walks to ensure the free flow of energy and remain energetic and healthy.

When we have a basic awareness of thoughts and subtle psychic energy, its relevance and importance, we can consciously regulate our nature of thoughts, emotions and energy levels, which are vital for our health and wellness. Only when we are aware can we give full attention to psychic energy and experience it.

We are by now aware that energetic feeling or mental energy or subtle energy is not sourced from our physical strength or calories alone. This can be substantiated from the fact that those who have suffered a stroke or undergone surgery experience fatigue and erosion of the subtle energy, but are recouped with more energy after a good sleep. Spiritually speaking, during sleep, we slip into the dimension of beingness and come in alignment or merge with the universal consciousness, which is the source of everything, including human consciousness. This inference can be further validated based on the experience of the deep meditators who can enhance their mental energy or subtle energy level through meditation when they reach a level of heightened awareness. So this higher level of awareness and the suggested practices will impact our subtle energy levels, which, in turn, impact our health and wellness, as well as our spiritual development and awakening.

We have seen that meditation plays a great role in maintaining higher energy levels, relaxing the brain, weakening the ego-mind-related brain circuits and reprogramming the subconscious mind. But, studies show that meditation has a lot of invaluable benefits to the body and mind, so we have to have a closer look at it.

10

WHY IS MEDITATION ESSENTIAL?

Meditation (*dhyan*) has been in practice in the East across all spiritual traditions since 1500 BCE, from the Vedic period. Yoga, which includes meditation as its inseparable part, has historical traces to even the pre-Vedic period. The scheme of yoga became systematized around the fifth and sixth centuries. Pathanjali synthesized and organized many traditions of yoga with a definite theoretical framework between 500 BCE and 400 BCE, which are known as the yoga sutras of Pathanjali.

The first World Parliament of Religions held in Chicago in 1893 helped spread awareness about meditation to the West. Due to the all-round benefits of yoga and meditation on health and wellness reported by various studies, it spread to the West very fast. The National Center for Complementary and Integrative Health states: 'Meditation is a mind and body practice that has a long history of use for increasing calmness and physical relaxation, improving physiological balance, coping with illness and enhancing overall health and well-being.' The National Health Interview Survey 2017 in USA reported that the practice of meditation by the adults there had tripled in the past 12 months.[1]

Nyanaponika Thera, a famous German Buddhist, states that if we observe our own minds, we shall notice how easily diverted our thoughts can be, how often they behave like undisciplined disputants constantly interrupting each other and refusing to listen to the other side's arguments.[2]

M.E. Raichle and others identified the default mode of brain functions in an article published under the title 'A Default Mode of Brain Function'.[3] This branch of neuroscience has gained importance in the recent past as studies found that most of the time, our default mode network (DMN) of brain circuits are active with the wandering mind and giving attention to the past or future, especially the immediate past and future.[4] It means DMN is the main brain network processing the ego-mind.

Every religion has taught some sort of meditative practice to evolve and achieve spiritual development. Today meditation techniques have spread across the world like wildfire, and many see it as a panacea for all their problems. Yet, many schools of science are sceptical about its benefits. However, many meditation practices, like transcendental meditation, have scientifically proven their benefits on all aspects of health and wellness.

Brain and Meditation

We know that the brain is the most unique and critical organ in the human body. There is a common perception that our brain needs rest and it gets some while we are not performing any activity. The vast majority of the circuits in the brain, especially the limbic brain, are involved in protecting, maintaining, strengthening the self and its identity—the so-called ego-mind, which drives 95 per cent of our lives. Hence, it is the brain's default mode. Generally, its thoughts, emotions and brain activities are negative and emotional in nature. Contrary to common belief, recent studies have revealed that the brain is fully activated when a person is doing nothing (as he then has a wandering mind), and when he is engaged in a constructive and focussed activity, most of the brain regions are deactivated and rested except the area involved in the specific activity. It has been observed that a wandering mind is a negative mind and is involved in a lot of brain activities, like nurturing, strengthening and reinforcing our ego-mind or false image. In short, when our attention is focussed deliberately on positive activities, our default negative mental activities are deactivated.

When a person is idle, the areas called MPFC and PCC are fully active. When we are engaged in constructive activity, only the corresponding area of the brain is activated; the above mentioned default areas are calmed down and rested. When a person meditates after a period of mind wandering, it is found that the neural circuits in PFC are strengthened, and this strengthening of neural circuits helps people reduce the mind wandering tendency. Dawson Church says, 'My studies show that meditators have higher volumes of brain tissues, better sleep, few diseases, increased immunity, enhanced emotional health, reduced inflammation, slower aging, increased intracellular communications, balanced neurotransmitters, greater longevity and less stress.'[5]

We know that there are many types of meditations available in the public domain. Some have a proven track record and benefits and are also immensely popular. The purpose of practising meditation is to focus our awareness and attention on the desired area of the mind or body or a specific activity. This process and the experience are called mindfulness.

'Sticking' and Meditation

Another feature of a wandering mind is its 'sticking' nature to certain types and patterns of thoughts. Depending upon the nature of self-image and perceptions of life, the mind develops a pattern of 'sticking' to certain types of thoughts and emotions, and develops a tendency to hang on to them. As the negative thoughts and emotions are repeated by way of sticking, they have a very harmful effect on the body and mind. The main cause of the mental conflict and pain of a person is this sticking nature of the mind, emotional attachment and resistance to different situations. These emotional aspects of the mind are regulated mainly by the amygdala and the nucleus accumbens. It is seen that meditation has the potential to reduce the grip of these regions on us and strengthen the rational thinking process.

It is also seen that the reduction of sticking nature helps reduce the intensity of the ego-mind, which helps people develop more connectedness to fellow human beings, feel compassion and undergo spiritual development. Meditation helps strengthen the dorsolateral prefrontal cortex of the brain, which is a key area involved in regulating negative thoughts, emotions and the ego-mind.

Meditation and Higher Awareness

Another astonishing finding of studies on meditation and mindfulness practice is that the long-term practice of the former helps raise the level of awareness amid practitioners. When practised for a longer period, the practitioners develop a higher level of awareness; that is, they become aware of their own awareness. This phenomenon is called meta-awareness, and this level of awareness can drastically reduce the grip of the default rigidity or false self of human beings. Similarly, long-term meditation practitioners have achieved a drastic and lasting reduction in mind wandering.

Emotional attachment, wandering mind, addictions, sense of false self and stickiness to thoughts and emotions are considered important traits of an ego-mind. It has been established that nucleus accumbens is involved in regulating these functions in the brain. In the case of long-term meditation practitioners, the grey matter volume attached to the nucleus accumbens diminishes substantially, which indicates the reduction in the intensity of the ego-mind and its adverse impacts. It means that there will be a corresponding increase in the experience of positive feelings of compassion and love in a natural way. Neuroscience has found that the brain structure alters according to the experience of a person. When long-term practitioners of meditation start experiencing more positive emotions, their brain circuits gradually change, paving the way for permanent changes in the brain structure.

Stress and Meditation

This is an era of stress, and there is widespread demand for various stress reduction programmes, especially in the West. Stress is identified as the root cause of many health problems. It is a proven fact that mindfulness meditation quickens the healing process. A study found that in the same situation, meditation practitioners release 13 per cent lesser cortisol, the stress hormone. They also experience a substantial reduction in pro-inflammatory cytokines. These are substantial changes that make a significant difference to a person's health.[6] It is well known that meditation can reduce blood pressure in a better way than medicine. It is reported that long-term practice of meditation can influence the gene expressions, especially inflammatory genes, indicating the prevention of many chronic illnesses, including mind-related ones. It also enhances the strength and longevity of cells.

Stress is an offshoot of a lifestyle driven by the ego-mind pattern or unconsciousness which is visible in all types of people; it spreads like wildfire, causing a threat to health and wellness. As various studies have shown that meditation gives a lot of relief against stress and related problems, modern society, especially in the West, has adopted different meditation practices, especially mindfulness-based meditation. Followed by Prof. Jon Kabat-Zinn's eight-week intensive mindfulness programme, called Mindfulness-Based Stress Reduction (MBSR) programme, many mindfulness-based programmes have started cropping up in the West. Cardiologist Herbert Benson found that meditation can change the thought pattern and stress response and result in health benefits like lowering of blood pressure level, heart rate, and help one attain deep relaxation.[7]

As the ego-mind's strategy is to deny the attention to and experience of the present moment, a critical goal of meditation becomes to be more and more anchored in the present moment with higher quality of attention. Dr Allan Wallace developed a meditation practice called Mindful Attention Training, focusing attention on breathing at a deeper level of awareness, which is reported to have a lot of benefits.[8]

Meditation, especially mindful attention, has shown many other benefits for our health. It helps us experience unavoidable physical pains with less emotional intensity, making them bearable. We have seen that the most severe problem faced by the modern-day man is negative emotional reactions to unfavourable situations, precisely stress. We have seen that long-term and repeated stressful situations cause severe health problems and are a serious area of concern for people in all walks of life. So people look for preventive or coping mechanisms against stress. Though much literature is available about the positive effects of meditation on avoiding or coping with stress, many have been sceptical and are looking for scientific evidence. Many studies have been conducted in the recent past, specifically on the role of meditation in modulating stress responses, emotional reactions and calming down the brain circuits connected to it. The amygdala is the brain's emotional radar. Though studies have reported a lot of positive and healthy neurological changes during meditation, it has also been found that a state of higher awareness and a tranquil mind are manifested and experienced in all aspects of life beyond the period of meditation.[9]

The brain pays attention to all the signals that are perceived as important, whether real or unreal, and creates fear or stress in response to threat signals. It triggers the emotional reaction and production of cortisol and adrenaline to put the body in an alert state to face stressful situations. It is found that people with constant experiences of stress have a longer amygdala and stronger circuits, and have a weak connection between the PFC and amygdala. During meditation, it has been noticed that the amygdala calms down and reduces the emotional reaction pattern. People who are meditation practitioners are found to have a smaller amygdala and stronger circuits between the PFC and the amygdala. Such people tend to recover to a balanced state of mind faster than non-practitioners.[10]

Neuroplasticity and Meditation

Studies found that experienced meditators recovere from stress situations more quickly than others or new meditators.[11] In the West, meditation practices are broadly categorized into two: focussed meditation and mindfulness meditation. The widely accepted definition of mindfulness is by Jon Kabat-Zinn. He defined it as, 'The awareness that emerges through paying attention on purpose, in the present moment and non-judgmentally to the unfolding of experience.'[12]

Once you decide to read this book, it means you are aware of your conflicts, pain, negative thoughts, emotions and behavioural patterns, and you have a deep urge to change or transform. We are aware that there is an option to have positive thoughts, lifestyle, good health and wellness in life, despite strong resistance from the ego-mind. The mind engineering process of this transformation is based on higher awareness, a life rooted in the present, and the deep experience of the reality that is the present moment. The most effective and precious supporting tool for this transformation process is meditation, which is time-tested and scientifically proven. The synaptic connections of a particular pathway doubles if we repeat the stimulation of having new experiences for one hour.13 All rich spiritual traditions of the world teach meditation for achieving a shift in awareness, healing, transcendence or salvation. The benefits of meditation are innumerable, are available free of cost, but are usually denied to us by the resistance from the ego-mind.

Meditation and health

The types of thoughts and attitudes play a role in maintaining the brain's health. People with a positive attitude of compassion and empathy have been found to have strengthened a critical area (between temporal and parietal lobes) in the brain. Being convinced of the miraculous benefits of meditation on health, American medical scientists have developed various practices, like mindfulness-based cognitive therapy (MBCT) for therapeutic purposes in cardiovascular diseases and mental illnesses. It has been observed that MBCT helps reduce relapse into severe depression by about 50 per cent.

A slow breath is an indicator of wellness and good health. It has been seen that long-term meditators take deeper breaths than non-meditators in the ratio of 1.6:1. Harvard scientists have found various critical regions of the brains of practitioners of meditation strengthening over a period. One study observed that the brains of meditators aged over 50 years were 'younger' by seven-and-a-half years compared to the non-meditators of the same age.[14] In another study, the brain of meditation practitioners aged 41 resembled the brain of 33 years old.[15]

Meditation and cognitive abilities

In the case of students, it has been noticed that mindfulness-based meditation has improved concentration and lessened mind wandering. It has also improved working memory, as they are able to pay more attention. One study reported a 30 per cent increase in the GRE scores of students who practiced mindfulness-based meditation compared to non-practitioners.[16]

Meditators reported higher levels of concentration and efficiency at work and more effective cognitive functions. Neuroscientists observed brain coherence involving all parts of the brain among meditators—the healthiest state of the brain. The gamma waves originated from the thalamus moved to the back of the brain, then to the front about 40 times per second. This indicates a peak level of mental and physical performance with alertness, awareness and concentration. The immune system also improves substantially among meditators. Nobel prize winner Francis Harry Compton Crick observed that the state of meditators' brains is the key to a higher level of cognition and positive qualities, like a higher level of intelligence, compassion, self-control, improvement in IQ, and improvements in overall physical and mental performance.[17] Increased memory power, better perception and processing of signals in the brain were observed in many meditators.

Meditation and mental health

Meditation helps achieve calmness and peace of mind, and also aids one in coming out of depression; brain activities in the left PFC, which are involved in self-control, happiness and compassion, are found to improve. It reduces activities of the amygdala, which is the regulator of mainly negative emotions and adrenaline-driven emotional activities. It also helps people experience love at a deeper level and improves the quality of all aspects of their life. Many meditators experienced a reduction of brain noise or mind chatter, and saw improvement in the mental energy level. At the brain level, new neurons are created, which enhances the its ability and quickens the body's healing process. It reduces stress, anxiety and panic tendencies, and improves the mental wellness of a person. We know that the left and right hemispheres of the brain have distinct functions, and their synchronized functioning is essential for the brain's effective working—this can be achieved through meditation. Higher qualities of the mind, like intention, inquisitiveness, visualization, creativity, experience of presence, higher awareness, mindful experiences, etc., are achieved in the case of long-term meditators.

Meditation and job efficiency

As benefits of meditation are experienced in all aspects of life, including job performance, many corporates have adopted mindfulness-based meditation practices as part of their training and development activities. Meditation rooms have been provided in many organizations in the recent past. In this modern era, many jobs have tough time-bound tasks, pressures and stress, which affect not only the efficiency but also the health and overall wellness of the human resources.

Studies found substantial improvement in efficiency level and organizational climate when mindfulness-based meditations were adopted. People of any age can start meditation at any time in their life.[18]

Meditation and reprogramming the mind

A lot of scientific studies have been conducted on the impact of meditation on brain circuits, and the following are the important findings:

i. Meditation reduces stress and weakens the emotional reaction circuits.
ii. It strengthens the brain circuits and improves the faculty of attention or focus.
iii. Brain circuits can be changed through intentional activities like meditation.[19] These changes are critical and helpful in moving forward towards transformation and improvement in one's quality of life.
iv. It improves the faculty of attention or focus.
v. It develops one's interest and positive attitude towards practising meditation.
vi. It helps to unwind the unhealthy programmes at the subconscious level, improve perceptions and create new synaptic connections in the brain, and achieve a higher level of consciousness and transformation. Experienced clinical psychologist, James Austin, addresses the benefit of Zen practices scientifically in his book titled *Zen and the Brain*.[20] He has also been practising Zen for three decades and has had a few mystical experiences too. He highlighted that Zen meditation practices help eliminate the neural structures of the ego-mind-centric network in the brain.[21]

vii. Meditators are found to have smaller nucleus accumbens, the circuit of which is associated with want or attachment. Such people help create a positive work environment and motivate others to follow suit. The quality of work at such a workplace will be of very high order.

The DMN of the brain creates a compulsive tendency to think and emotionally react to the past and future, further strengthening the ego-mind patterns. We have seen that the ego-mind is very strong and will use all the resources and intelligence available to strengthen itself by way of creating conflict, stress and pain. The ego-mind misuses our brain's unique part, the neocortex area—it has evolved over many generations and makes human beings unique with higher qualities and experiences like rational thinking, decision-making skills, organizing capabilities, higher spiritual awareness, etc. The PFC, located just behind the forehead, has unique qualities, like drawing past knowledge and experiences and making reasonable anticipation about the future to enrich the present and make preparation and plan for making the future more meaningful. But the ego-mind misuses these abilities and utilizes them to 'relive' in the past with negative emotional reactions, creating worries and anxieties about the future, thus, serving it's purpose. But it has been observed that mindfulness practices reduce the amygdala activities involving the emotional reactions, weaken stress circuits and strengthen the networks that enable a higher quality of attention to the present.[22]

Meditation and Attention

After survival, our goal is a higher quality of life, which means quality of experiences, and that depends on the quality of our attention. This is applicable in every aspect of life. Enjoying tasty food depends on the quality of attention we are giving to it. Zen meditations give more importance to attention. When a student asked a Zen master for a one-word mantra for success, he answered, 'Attention'. When the student insisted on clarity, he said, 'Attention is attention.'[23] But attention enjoys a predominant place in all types of meditation. In 1890, William James highlighted the importance of attention in his *Principles of Psychology* and said, 'An education which should improve this faculty would be the education par excellence.' The functional efficiency of every activity depends on the alertness and attention we give it. As 'attention' is of paramount importance in the quality of our lives, many studies were conducted in this field and conclusively found that it helps us avoid distraction and strengthens our ability to be alert and focussed. The neural circuits for selective attention can be trained and maintained, helping us find a solution to the wandering mind.[24]

In modern society, people, especially those in the technical field, are required to be multitaskers with a high propensity to stress and the need for concerted efforts. The ability of concentrated attention is weakened in a multitasking environment, and it is further worsened with health impacts when stress is added. This situation adversely affects the overall efficiency, health and wellness of the workforce in the long run. Hence, many corporates turn towards meditation as an effective solution to these problems. Different meditation practices, including mindfulness training, have proved to be effective for multitaskers.

Meditation and Breath

Many meditation practices are linked with observing breathing patterns. Counting one's natural breaths for 10 minutes and observing its flow with closed eyes is very effective for immediate relaxation and regaining cognitive control.[25] A study reported that an eight-minute session on mindful breathing and attention lessened the mind-wandering activity afterward.[26] When we are able to observe our own mental activities, we gain control over them without being driven away by them. The great philosopher Sam Harris said, 'That which is aware of sadness is not sad. That which is aware of fear is not fearful. The moment I am lost in thought, however, I'm as confused as anyone else.'[27]

When we practise meditation for a long period of time with higher spiritual or mind engineering wisdom, we can give attention to our mind activities, like thoughts, emotions, compulsive patterns and desires. This would lead us to the highest level of awareness—meta-awareness—wherein we would become aware of our own awareness, which is a state of awakening.

Our attention's quality depends upon the nature of the situations and brain areas involved in paying attention and triggering the reactions. When there is an immediate life-threatening situation, our brainstem will react to protect ourselves in the default mode without much thinking. When we pay attention to a stressful situation by emotionally reacting to it, our amygdala in the limbic brain gets involved, triggering various body functions. When a person with meditation practice faces such stressful situations, he bypasses these circuits, as PFC circuits are stronger and react rationally to it.

The higher wisdom and awareness from this mind engineering journey have strengthened the brain networks through meditation, promoting a rational approach, focussed attention and experience of the present moment, which can be sustained when we practise it daily.

Meditation and Longivity

Many studies report the effects of the state of mind on illness, health and healing. Inflammatory agents or genes have a great impact on the body, triggering many serious illnesses. It was found that there is considerable down-regulation of inflammatory genes in the case of meditators. Studies have reported the epigenetic impact of meditation on genes. Sense of loneliness promotes pro-inflammatory genes, but it was found that mediation lowers pro-inflammatory genes and the adverse impact of loneliness on human body.[28]

The telomere's length, the end cap of the DNA strand, is directly proportional to the length of the lifespan of cells, and the telomerase enzyme decides the age of the telomere. It was found that in the case of meditators, there is an increased activity for the protection of telomerase.[29] Slower and deeper breathing is an indicator of health and longevity of lifespan. It is found that compared to non-meditators, mediation practitioners are able to heave deeper breath.[30] Meditators have been found to have thicker cortex areas that are related to higher faculties, like paying attention and higher awareness.[31] Another encouraging report came from a study of University of California, Los Angeles, which reported that in the case of long-term meditators, the brain's age-related shrinkage slows down. Among 50-year-olds who practised mindfulness-based meditation, their brains were found to be younger by seven-and-a-half years compared to those of non-meditators.[32] Mindfulness-based therapies have been found to be more effective than drugs for people suffering from depression.[33]

Meditation can enable focussed activities and deactivation of the emotional limbic brain. It helps us calm down the brain and mind and anchor ourselves in the present. Meditation enables heightened awareness and experience of the present moment. We can restructure or remodel our brains depending upon our type and nature of thoughts, emotions and the quality of our attention.

Meditation also facilitates liberation from the addictive and compulsive patterns of thoughts and emotions and helps experience an altered state of consciousness. Throughout the practice, a higher level of awareness can be experienced, leading to a sustained transformation.

Meditation, a Precious Gift

As meditation is a precious gift available free of cost and the most important tool for reprogramming the subconscious mind, transformation and awakening, we cannot afford to ignore it; we must commit to practise it regularly without yielding to the distractions or resistance of the ego-mind. It is also our moral responsibility to disseminate this wisdom to others. Many different types of meditations are taught, practised and also available in the public domain to follow. You are advised to practise meditation meticulously. In addition to that, we need to have a shift in awareness about everything in life; we should not get engaged in the addictive tendencies of the linear world. We can practise being in a meditative state, even for a few minutes, by rooting ourself in the following ways:

i. We can refocus our attention to the sensory signals, like seeing an object and experiencing it in its fullest spiritual dimension, without a wandering mind.
ii. We can observe the coming thoughts without judgement, increase the gap between thoughts, and have glimpses of liveliness in between.

iii. We can observe the flow of our breath as we inhale and exhale.
iv. We can lie down in savasana and shift our attention from head to toes, slowly visualizing a healthy body and internal organs and feel the subtle body energy that has a profound effect on health and our overall wellness.
v. We can observe a thought and our breaths alternatively.
vi. We can frequently ask ourselves 'where is my attention?' and focus our attention on every little activity with full awareness and experience—this is a powerful mindfulness practice.

Being aware of its invaluable benefits in all aspects of our life, a rational person cannot afford to ignore or avoid daily meditation. Its benefits will be experienced in the family, workplace and society where you are interacting with people, and it should be your resolution and firm commitment to practise it every day. Meditation can also accelerate the healing process; not only meditation, our positive mind, which is liberated from the control of the ego-mind, has tremendous healing power. We will explore that now.

11

HEALING POWER OF THE MIND

We have seen that our body consciousness is a state of unconsciousness, and this unconsciousness complements physical illnesses. The rigidity of the ego-mind and body consciousness are complementary to each other. Soul consciousness helps us remain healthy and heal fast. Not only does an engineered, reprogrammed and awakened mind help us stay in good health and promote wellness, it also has tremendous healing power.

Modern medical science says that the mind causes more than 90 per cent of the illnesses;[1] if the mind can cause illnesses, it can also heal. We have seen that we are transceivers; we send out signals to the environment and also receive signals. As most of the signals received by the cells are from the environment, and the cell functions are influenced by these signals, a branch of science has emerged, namely the science of signal transduction, which studies the influence of environmental signals on organisms. It recognizes the fact that the fate and behaviour of organisms, including human beings, are directly linked to the way they perceive the environmental signals.

We have been taught that our body functions and health are programmed in the genes, so we believe that we are the victims of our fate. But recently, science has found that most gene expressions happen based on the nature of signals received from the environment, which help us have a paradigm shift in our belief that we are masters of our own destiny. Biologist H.F. Nijhout says, 'When a gene product is needed, a signal from its environment, not an emergent property of the gene itself, activates expression of that gene.' Studies show that only 5 per cent of cardiovascular and cancer patients have genetic roots of their illness.[2] There is a tendency to attribute the cause of illness to the gene, which is wrong; 95 per cent of us get diseases due to our pattern of thinking, feeling and lifestyle, and this has been validated by many studies in the recent past.[3] Our genes are influenced by the way we interact with people, face life situations and experiences. It is found that 90 per cent of our genes respond in cooperation with signals received from the environment.[4] Understanding this fact, Earnest Rossi, says, 'Our subjective states of mind, consciously motivated behaviour, and our perception of free-will can modulate gene expression to optimize health.'[5] The perception and beliefs of the subconscious mind create an energy field that sends signals to the body as per its nature, and the body manifests it and creates the physical reality. The environmental signals include predominantly the thoughts and emotions, which are in accordance with our subconscious mind programme. When we identify with the ego-mind, we are driven by our subconscious mind most of the time. As a result of this, most of the thoughts and emotions are negative, which manifests in our body and life.

With higher awareness, we can change our subconscious mind programme and the old pattern of thoughts, emotions and lifestyle to get the life we want. A deeper understanding of body functions at the cellular level and the importance of thoughts will help us attain a higher awareness and affect the reprogramming at the subconscious mind level.

We know that our basic biological unit is the cell, and each cell has thousands of integral membrane proteins (IMP), called receptors. These are protein nanoparticles functioning as sensors or mini antennae to receive signals from the environment. There are broadly two categories of these receptors: receptor proteins and effector proteins. When a signal is sensed, corresponding receptor proteins attract to it and 'bind' to that particular signal, like a lock fitting its key. This causes changes in the protein's electrical charges, resulting in changes to the shape of proteins, which adopt an active position, leading to the production of required protein and cell behaviour. There are receptor proteins that respond to physical signals too. For example, an estrogen receptor, which is programmed to sense estrogen, locks on to it, like a magnet. The electromagnetic charge of the receptor results in an active position that passes on the signals through effector proteins inside the cells for corresponding functions and expression of genes and production of proteins to carry out the required physical functions. Many receptors can sense the energy fields and signals from outside, like light, sound, thoughts, emotions, etc., and carry out corresponding functions.

Oxford University physicist, C.W. McClare, carried out a detailed study and compared the efficiency between energy signals and chemical signals (drugs) in the biological systems. His findings were published with the title 'Resonance in bioenergetics' in the journal called *Annals of New York Academy of Science*.[6] This study revealed that the energetic signalling mechanisms are a hundred times more efficient at passing on environmental signals to the cells than physical signals, such as neurotransmitters, growth supplements, hormones, chemical substances, etc.[7] Conventional medicine did not accept the finding seriously, which may be due to the influence of the pharmaceutical industry. How the change of thoughts and mindset affects health has been described by N. Cousin, who has shown that regular laughter sessions could heal even chronic illness.[8] The influence of the mind on the body has been under study over decades, and a new branch of science called psychoneuroimmunology (PNI) has been developed to study the healing effect of the mind on the body.

Different Perspective of Healing

When the mind engineering process envisages awakening and transformation, it also brings higher awareness and quality of life. Spiritual science and body-mind science have given a new dimension and approach towards healing. Scientific studies have reported many instances of incurable diseases getting cured with the power of the mind.

Modern science, including medical science, is based on the Newtonian materialistic view. There has always been another school that believed that a person is a spiritual being. In the recent past, with the advent of quantum physics, a gradual shift is taking place in understanding everything in the universe, including human beings and consciousness. This paradigm shift in understanding human beings has also changed the approach towards healing. A human being is perceived not as a combination of different parts, but is seen with a holistic approach. Quantum physics says everything is energy in different forms, and vibrations and consciousness is the basic building block of everything, including the so-called material things in the universe. At the individual level, consciousness is not the product of the brain; on the contrary, consciousness is the coordinating and driving force of all body functions, even at the minute cellular level. Recent cellular biology tells us that the basic building block of human beings and their activities are proteins in the cells, which are expressed as per the signals received mostly from the environment—especially perceptions, thoughts and emotions—and not from the genetic codes or programmes. The environment mainly includes mind and consciousness, among other physical environmental factors. Due to these developments in science, alternative medicine and treatment methods, like energy medicine and healing with the power of mind, are gaining importance and acceptance.

Mind, in short, means the way we think and feel. A study by the Harvard Medical School reported that a positive outlook is the strongest protection against heart diseases.[9] There are many scientific reports on the power of the mind or change in perceptions leading to eradication of incurable diseases, including cancer. Many recent authors say that the body is the manifestation of our mind, and both cannot be seen as separate entities. It was found that thoughts of optimism and hope resulted in the production of more dopamine.[10] To put it in a simple example, if the body is like a product in a factory, the important raw materials are our subconscious mind's thoughts and emotions.

Modern science tells us that cells respond to the environment, including thoughts and emotions, more than the genetic factors. Biochemists tell us that negative thoughts and emotions produce various substances in the body that are harmful to health, and at the same time, positive thoughts, emotions and stress-free life produce various substances that are healthy and facilitate healing. When about 90 per cent thoughts are similar every day, and 70–80 per cent are negative, the same raw materials are used to make the product daily, i.e., for the creation of similar cells and the maintenance of the body as it was. But, here we can see an opportunity or window for healing with the power of the mind.

Every day, a major part of our body is replaced following the cell division process. The huge factory of the human body, which has about 40 trillion cells, produces new cells every second. The body produces one trillion new red blood cells per day.[11] Every second, more than eight lakh cells are created; about 60 million new cells are produced in the day.[12] But as the main raw material is the same, i.e., same thoughts and emotions, the same products are produced. If we want to improve the quality of the product, we have to improve the quality of the raw material, i.e., the thoughts, emotions, lifestyle, in short, perceptions and beliefs of the mind. This is the secret window nature has provided us to make healthy changes in the body or heal; this is how healing takes place with the power of the mind. It is reported that many fighters of breast cancers are healed by the mind and body without the intervention of any treatment.[13] A similar percentage is reported in the case of cancer affecting white blood cells.[14] From the review of medical reports, in 1993, there were about 3,000 cases of spontaneous remission of cancers.[15]

Different alternative medicines or healing methods, like positive psychology, energy medicine, meditation, hypnotic suggestions, etc., which help people send positive signals to the body to heal, have started gaining acceptance in the recent past. In many instances of NDE, people reported total transformation of their perceptions and experience of unconditional love, which even resulted in the healing of incurable diseases, like cancer. The mind engineering approach of healing is based on these scientifically proven principles. It helps people channel their mind power to heal themselves. Healing is a natural process that is blocked by our negative mind patterns. If we remove these blocks, healing can take place naturally; when it is coupled with belief, right intentions and healthy practices, like meditation, the healing process picks up pace. It is reported that even positive belief alone results in the production of endorphins, which are natural painkillers.[16]

Hypnotic suggestions help a person bypass the subconscious mind signals and experience deep relaxation, rejuvenation and high energy levels, and experience the healing process. If we can change the basic perceptions at the subconscious mind level and help a person have a higher awareness about self, others, life, world, mediation, healthy lifestyle and believe in healing with the power of the mind, it can result in miraculous healing. I have known a person suffering from chronic hypophosphatemia who was assisted by mind engineering wisdom in getting completely healed.[17] Psychologist Jeanne Achterberg used the intention and visualization method to cure the cancer in her eye.[18]

The entire healing process can be summarized with the help of an example of TV. Suppose one channel, A, always telecasts harmful and negative programmes; another channel, B, always shows healthy and joyous programs. If we are tuning the TV for channel A, it will always telecast unhealthy programmes, like our present life driven by the ego-mind; channel A is already tuned and set as the default channel. If we can change the tuning to the channel B and allow it to manifest, it will show a healthy and happy programme. But unconsciously, as we have set channel A as the default channel, the programmes manifested will be negative and unhealthy.

Now, let us come to our life, which is driven by the subconscious mind programme. When a large number of negative thoughts and patterns are repeated every day, we are strengthening the same neural pathways and structures in the brain most of the time and creating the same emotions, experiences and biochemistry. As specified before, it is estimated that 75–85 per cent of the genes expressed are based on the environment's signals, including thoughts, beliefs, perceptions and emotions. Each half of the DNA zipper contains corresponding nucleic acid, and groups of the long sequences of these nucleic acids are called genes. In the normal course, DNA in the cell contains information regarding what we are and who we are going to be, and the DNA keeps sending signals to produce protein and manifest these perceptions and beliefs—the mind on the body. So, in order to bring about positive changes in the body or heal, we need to make corresponding new proteins in the cells. For that purpose, we have to send new healthy and positive signals to genes; to do so, we will have to change our perceptions, beliefs, thoughts, emotions and lifestyle. The production and expression of new proteins and their manifestations will give new experiences to the brain, and new connections and circuits will be created, which will change our old patterns of thought, feelings and behaviours, sustainably facilitating the change or healing.

Eric Kandel reports that the brain wants new experiences, and when it has new experiences, it produces double the number of synaptic connections than usually done by repeated experiences.[19] When new experiences are repeated, the new structure is created, and it rewrites our old subconscious programme, which leads to positive changes in a permanent manner.

The mind and body do not differentiate between real or unreal beliefs. For example, people under hypnotic trance can develop blisters when touched with a cold iron rod when told that it is a hot rod. So when we believe something a 100 per cent, e.g., a healed body, and visualize and experience the healed state, it sends corresponding signals to cells' genes and produces corresponding new proteins, and manifests a healed body. The brain also believes in such a visualized experience as real and makes corresponding neural changes in the brain's structure and facilitates sustainable changes in thoughts, feelings and behavioural patterns.

The genetic information recorded in the genes can be rewritten by a change in belief, perception and new experiences. This phenomenon is called epigenetics. It is estimated that less than 5 per cent of people are born with genetic health issues,[20] and 90 per cent of the genes respond to signals from the environment.[21] The environment includes our thoughts, emotions, perception, and beliefs. Prof. Rossi writes: 'Our subjective states of mind, consciously motivated behaviour, and our perception of free will modulate gene expression to optimize health.'[22] Some scientists say that we usually express only 1.5 per cent DNA, and a balance of 85.5 per cent is called junk DNA.[23]

Out of the internal and external elements in the environment affecting the body, the most important are the experiences, which depend on the meaning we attribute to various signals. It means that there is a tremendous possibility of affecting gene expressions, physical changes and healing by bringing about a change in how we think, feel and behave.

Healing with Belief

There are many medical reports of healing of so-called incurable diseases with the power of mind and belief. A famous and typical case was reported in 1952. Dr Albert Mason, who used to heal patients with certain types of illnesses using hypnotic suggestions, tried to heal a 15-year-old boy suffering from skin warts, which was extreme and chronic, and the boy found it difficult to lead a normal life.[24] Dr Mason and other doctors used hypnosis to treat warts. The boy was referred to Dr Mason by a surgeon who found it difficult to treat the boy with surgery as the nature of the disease was unusually outgrown. After a few hypnosis sessions, the boy was healed, and Dr Mason later discussed the case with the surgeon; it was revealed that the boy was referred for a hypnosis session by mistake. It was a wrong diagnosis, and after detailed clinical examinations, it was found that it was not a case of skin warts, but a confirmed case of congenital ichthyosis, which is an incurable skin disease!

Healing with the belief or placebo has gained acceptability in science. But the term 'placebo' was often referred in a negative connotation of fake feeling or nescience, and reductionist science debunked it. However, there are a lot of studies that prove healing by placebo. It was reported that the effect of pain relief and healing happen due to placebo effect, and it resulted in the development of a branch of science called the neurobiology of placebo.[25] Irving Kirsch, PhD, a psychologist at the University of Connecticut, conducted a study involving 2,300 patients with depression and found that most improvements were due to belief, not due to antidepressants.[26] Kirsch and his team held another detailed study based on 35 clinical trials on various antidepressants and found that placebos worked well 81 per cent of the time.[27]

Famous biologist and author Lewis Thomas says that healing with the power of mind or belief, like the healing of skin warts, is 'one of the great mystifications of science', as biologically, the healing process involves a lot of intricate activities at the cellular level. He concluded that there must be a 'person in charge, kind of super-intelligence in all of us...infinitely smarter and possessed of technical know-how far beyond our present understanding.'[28] Another study found that placebos are not just improved feeling; they actually change the brain wave patterns.[29] Researchers of University of British Columbia, Vancouver, found a 200 per cent increase in dopamine among Parkinson's patients when they were administered a placebo, telling them that it was a special drug.[30]

Many studies have found that the belief and intention of the mind to heal even heals incurable diseases or spontaneous remissions.[31] In a detailed study of 2,318 clinical drug trials for antidepressant medications, it was found that 50.97 per cent of healings were due to mental belief and intention to heal.[32]

Mind over Matter

Though it is a fact that there are many instances of incurable illnesses having healed with the power of the mind, it does not mean that every single positive thought from our conscious mind will have healing effect all the time. We can think positively from our conscious mind, but the perceptions and beliefs of the subconscious mind are stronger and have an overriding effect on the thoughts of our conscious mind. The thoughts will have a healing effect on our body only if we have 100 per cent belief in them, unconditionally at our subconscious mind level, like in the case of hypnotic suggestion.

We have seen that the subconscious mind programme supersedes the conscious mind's needs, desires, thoughts, ideas and images in the normal course. Hence, the positive thoughts with the healing objective may not give the desired result, as the ego-mind resists any change induced by the conscious mind.

All signals, including thoughts generated by the conscious mind, are interpreted by the ego-mind first before making sense, and conclusions of such signals are drawn and registered deep in the mind. So, the positive thoughts or signals for healing should be unconditional and undoubted belief and an intention from a state of higher awareness without the ego-mind's interpretation. Many illnesses are healed or physical changes are manifested through hypnotic suggestions, as these are received directly into the subconscious mind without interpretation or doubt or resistance of the conscious mind.

We have seen that our biochemistry depends on our thoughts, emotions and beliefs. During a hypnotic trance, the body changes as per the suggestions given; for example, muscles can be hardened or relaxed instantaneously based on the suggestions. Certain yogis and Zen masters have shown miraculous control and changes in the body with mind power. Another way the mind influences the body is through firm belief, using which our brain can produce chemical substances or medicines to heal our body. As said, studies have proved that placebos were as effective as antidepressants in the case of depression patients. This was evident in clinical trials of many medicines. In one study, depression patients were given sumatriptan to control cortisol and stimulate growth hormones, and the drug was replaced with a placebo without intimating the patients. But it was surprising that the brain scan showed same changes as in the case of the drug.[33]

Energy Medicine

Descartes held the view that mind and body exist in separate realms and dismissed the idea that the mind influences the body. He believed that matter could affect matter, and the immaterial mind could not influence the material body. The conventional medical science, which was based on Descartes's philosophy, reported instances of miraculous healings, terming them as 'exceptions'. This mind and matter division created by Descartes's philosophy and Newtonian physics has been undone and reconnected by quantum physics, which postulates that everything is energy in different frequencies and vibrations, including the so-called material things.

The latest findings of quantum physics tell us that there is a field of immense energy, information and potential, which is the source of every thing, and every thing exists within this field. It implies that the energy field influences the matter; at the individual level, mental energy influences the physical body. It is found that the human energy field regulates body functions and it also has healing potential.[34] It gives a more effective healing protocol and wider scope for alternative treatments, like energy medicine.

When a person is inactive, he produces 10–15 millivolts of electrostatic energy; during activities of focussed attention, like meditation, it surges up to 3 volts; during the energy healing process, it goes up to 190 volts.[35] This validates the distance energy healing.[36]

Science has found that all living things emanate light or energy. Studies also found that a stream of light flowed out of the dominant hands of energy healers with the intention to heal.[37] Stanford University physicist, William A. Tiller, found that intended and directed thoughts transfer physical energy without relevance to the distance, validating distance energy healings. Energy healing happens when the healer sends energy of intention along with the power of mind. Human beings are receivers and transmitters of quantum energy or signals; directed intention appears to show electrical and magnetic energy stream photons changing the molecular structure of matter.[38] A large study that included 1,000 graduates confirmed that energy healing works.[39]

Dr Dispenza believes that there's an intelligence, an invisible consciousness, within each of us and that's the giver of life. It supports, maintains, protects and heals us every moment.[40] Modern quantum mechanics and science also endorse this fact, which says that everything is energy in different vibrational frequencies, and everything, including individual consciousness, exists in a field of higher potential, energy and information (cosmic consciousness).

Energy Healing

Energy healing means 'any purely mental effort undertaken by one person with the intention of improving physical or emotional well-being of another'.[41] Electromagnetic signals from the environment are received by the receptors, the signal receiving antennae located on the cell membrane. Corresponding signals in the form of proteins are sent to the nucleus of cells, and these signals look for specific chromosome which contains the genes, just like we look for a particular book in a library. Each chromosome contains DNA strands that are covered by another type of protein. The cover or sleeve is to be removed so that the DNA becomes accessible to the signal, like accessing the selected book from a shelf in the library. Depending on the nature of the signal, the corresponding DNA will open up to produce corresponding proteins. When DNA is opened, RNA is produced outside the nucleus to be assembled into new proteins called amino acids, which are the body's building blocks. RNA is a blueprint with a lot of potentials. So, the energy-based healing practices gained momentum and more acceptance in the recent past. In a review of 90 studies, it was found that the energy healing techniques were effective in two-third of instances.[42]

Allan Cooperstein, a clinical and forensic psychologist of Saybrook Graduate School, found scientific evidence of success in energy healing. Researchers found amazing mind power achieved by Buddhist monks; they could raise their body temperature up to 9.4°C and lower metabolism by 60 per cent with the power of the mind.[43] In 1939, S.D. Kirlian photographed the electromagnetic field of human beings, human 'aura'.[44] Scientists Schwartz and Great developed images of light activity emanating from living things. They found a stream of light flowing from the dominant hands and fingers of energy healers while performing distant energy healing. William Tiller invented a device to measure the energy produced by healers and found that there is a substantial increase in the energy level in the body while transmitting healing energy over a large distance. So our perceptions and experiences send signals to the cell. The brain also responds to such signals, and synaptic connections are formed as per the nature of experiences. Our experience depends on our perceptions and beliefs of the subconscious mind, which interprets various signals and attributes meaning and creates corresponding experiences. Healthy and positive experiences can effect positive changes in the body, including healing. When we are under stress, the result is opposite.

Positive Mind (Love) and Healing

We have seen that negative thoughts and emotions are the sources of most illnesses. When we live in the negative zone, the body stays in protective mode and our ability to heal reduces drastically. As said earlier, it implies that if the negative mind is causing illness, a positive mind can heal. The most fundamental positive feeling is love. It is often said that the basic nature of divinity is unconditional love. The term 'love' is often understood in a limited sense, but it has deeper dimensions. The innate feeling of unconditional and pure love is the manifestation of our consciousness as human experiences. We have seen that there are many instances of people who healed themselves from incurable or chronic illnesses after facing NDE or OBE. Most of such people highlighted their experience of unconditional pure love, which led to their healing.

Practise Healing with the Power of Mind

Based on studies of ancient religious wisdom and modern science, the following critical wisdom can be used for healing with the power of the mind.

When we are under stress and cells are in the protective or survival mode, communications and signals are interrupted, and healing gets delayed. Healing takes place fast only when we are in growth mode, which means when we are relaxed with a positive frame of mind. The communication between cells, production of proteins in the cells, signals to the stem cells to transform into required cells take place effectively only when the signals and communications are clear and uninterrupted. So meditation has the potential to heal our body and mind.

For practical guidance on healing with the power of the mind, the following process is involved:

i. We should have clear awareness that we are identified fully with the ego-mind, and this ego-mind drives our thoughts, emotions and lifestyle. Our perception and beliefs of the subconscious mind are manifesting in our thoughts, feelings, action, physique, health and mind. With this higher awareness, we will no longer be slaves of the ego-mind.

ii. Now we have a deep awareness that we are pure living consciousness with human experiences and form part of a larger consciousness, in the form of condensed energy, which is all-powerful and has full potential to change or heal the body.

iii. We need undoubted, deep, clear awareness and belief that our body or most of our illness is a manifestation of our mind, and so, it can be changed with changes in the mind (thoughts, emotions, beliefs and perception).
iv. With the above awareness, the ego-mind needs to be inactive and we need a calm state of mind, like the one we have when in a state of meditation or trance. Then we need to visualize that we are healed and experience the healed state of the body; feel corresponding emotions and gratitude associated with the state of healed body. The best time for this practice is just before falling asleep or waking up.

Can we experience a future event? We can only experience the now. When we visualize with a 100 per cent belief, create corresponding emotions and experience as if it is happening or has happened, the body, including the brain and mind, cannot differentiate between real and unreal situations. It will express gene functions, change brain structure (neuroplasticity), and affect changes in the body. It also applies in the case of healing. When you add joy and gratitude with the visualization and an experience of having a healed body, it will deepen and quicken the manifestation and changes. When this visualization is repeated, the neurons fired together get wired together, and it will reinforce the changes and bring results.

Language of the Mind

Whatever the body and mind pay attention to, it grows and improves. The mind understands the language expressing a state of mind or a situation or an activity mainly in the present tense. If one says, 'I will not have stage fear', the mind gives attention to stage fear, and it will manifest. On the contrary, if one says, 'I am confident while speaking', confidence is given attention to, and mind will manifest confidence while speaking. If one frequently says, 'I don't want to be sick', attention is given to sickness, and he will fall sick. If one says, 'I am healthy', he will remain healthy. If one say, 'I will be healed', it indicates the future, which is not a reality, and it will not happen. If we believe and say, 'I am healed and healthy' with belief, the body will experience and manifest it.

If we fully believe something, even if it is not real, the subconscious mind, brain and the entire body will bring about corresponding changes, including healing. We have seen this fact from the hypnotic suggestions to the subconscious mind when the conscious mind is not active. The visualization and affirmation techniques can be used effectively for various purposes, including excellence in sports. This vital fact will help us when we try to achieve many things with the power of the mind, including healing.

12

REPROGRAMMING OF SUBCONSCIOUS MIND

Now we are at a critical stage, at a turning point in the journey towards transformation and awakening through the mind engineering process. After being fully aware of life's goal and all aspects of the obstacles and blockades in our way towards awakening, we are at a stage to show our commitment and responsibility to put the wisdom into practice or change our old ego-mind patterns practically. We know that it is an urgent need and a medical emergency. With higher awareness about all this wisdom, we have already achieved a shift in awareness and perceptions on different aspects of life. We have changed a lot and prepared ourselves to do systematic reprogramming and follow certain practices that will reinforce new wisdom and create new experiences that will make corresponding changes in the brain circuits and make the resulting changes a sustainable one.

Mind engineering process of reprogramming the subconscious mind follows a holistic approach of human beings, including body, mind and consciousness. It is founded on the following basic premises:

i. Higher awareness of all aspects of human beings,
ii. Selective full attention to reality, the present moment and
iii. Full experience of reality, the present

We have become deeply aware of all vital aspects of human beings, especially mind and consciousness. Awareness about the ego-mind will weaken its supporting brain circuits, strength and its control on us. Our awareness about consciousness, different conscious practices like meditation and other reprogramming methods will facilitate new patterns and approaches to life, and strengthening of brain circuits facilitating new experiences. With higher awareness, we are able to observe the dynamics and manifestations of the ego-mind. This holistic approach will result in gradually weakening the ego-mind, its control on us and strengthen our true self. When we continue to follow these practices and new experiences with commitment and responsibility, changes will happen at the level of:

i. Shift in awareness in the subconscious mind,
ii. Changes in the brain circuits,
iii. Changes in the biochemistry,
iv. Changes in everyday life experiences, accompanied by better health and wellness, and
v. Strengthening of true self and spiritual development

'Silver-Bullet' Methods Have Limitations

There are many short-term methods and practices people that adopt to have positive thoughts and emotions in the place of negative ones or, in short, transform from the negative zone to the positive zone. But studies by various scientists, like Miriam Rothschild[1] and Joseph E. LeDoux[2], show that such short-term methods without a holistic approach, without resorting to proper reprogramming of the subconscious mind and without evolving spiritually, will have only very limited results. After extensive study, Hilary Stokes and Kimberly Ward in their book,

The Happy Map: Your Roadmap to the Habit of Happiness, stated: 'There is not one strategy that leads to happiness; it results from dedication to a holistic—or mind, body, and spirit—approach. It takes focus, effort, and intention on a daily basis. This is where the real results come from.'[3]

Subconscious Mind Programme

In the mind engineering process, we need to have basic awareness about the existing subconscious mind programme. This programme is the foundation of our ego-mind, and it creates an image of ourselves, our personality, and we believe in it. As the vast majority of our emotional experiences of childhood are negative, the ego-mind's basic nature is negative, manifesting negative thoughts and emotions. When we grow up and have similar experiences, (or believed to have), the emotional self or baggage grows to a mammoth size and strengthens the supporting hardwired brain circuits. Our conscious mind, which becomes aware of lots of mental pain, conflicts, problems and consequences in life, wishes to end all of it, but feels helpless. The conscious mind will have a lot of wishes and desires, but the very strong subconscious mind succeeds and prevails. We are usually unaware of the subconscious mind programme and live individually and collectively in a state of unconsciousness or 'darkness'. So reprogramming our subconscious mind is the essential need to move further in the journey towards transformation and awakening.

Origin of the Programme

We have seen that the origin of the subconscious programme lies in the early childhood experiences and the conclusions drawn. So the people involved in taking care of us during our childhood and their behavioural patterns critically influence our lives. If parents have rigid ego-mind patterns, it will have a tremendous impact on children's subconscious mind programmes, behavioural patterns and their overall personality.

We have seen that one strategy of a dense ego-mind is to control others. Suppose parents, either one or both, had suppressed, hurt or neglected childhood; they would have developed a rigid ego-mind with a tendency to be excessively controlling of their children and others in their family. They tend to have rigid norms for everything, and insist that others follow those. The ego-mind is aware that when rigid norms are forced upon others, there will always be conflicts and pain, and the ego-mind's position remains unchallenged. No child or adult likes to follow strict norms or be micromanaged on every frivolous thing—this creates hurt, resentment and pain. Children usually do not express it but the negative emotions created are stored in mind and get hardened when similar experiences are repeated. We have seen that everyone does not react the same way in same life situations; even within the same family and with the same parents, two children will not react to the situation in the same way; while one might develop a rebellious nature, the other might develop introversion or low self-esteem.

When such children grow up, their personalities will be dominated by a similar programme; behavioural patterns and the ego-mind will start playing the same tactics of insisting on rigid norms or micromanaging their children or family members; the history is repeated through generations unless the mind engineering wisdom is brought in to break it.

Can We Really Change?

The longest personality study focussed on 1,208 people from the age of 14 years to 77 years with periodical review and found that most of the beliefs and personality traits had totally changed over the years.[4] It emphasizes that if we take responsibility and, with higher awareness, we can change fundamentally. The feeling that we cannot change is nothing but a strategy of the ego-mind to resist change. Meditation weakens the amygdala network, which triggers negative emotional reactions, and strengthens the circuits of PFC, which modulates the activities of the amygdala and facilitates positive changes.

Need of Commitment and Responsibility

We have seen that resistance to change is very strong, and neuronal circuits processing the subconscious programme are much stronger than the part of the brain processing conscious mind and our true self. So higher awareness, strong will and commitment are essential to tide over the strong resistance of the subconscious mind and effect reprogramming and transformation. The awareness of the stiff resistance, various strategies played by the ego-mind and awareness about the urgency of change will help us commit ourselves to reprogramme and change. So, the most effective and natural way to change is by bringing the light of higher awareness and wisdom at the experiential level within. When we bring more awareness and give more attention to every moment and activity, we will have new experiences.

Reprogramming the Subconscious Mind

We have shifted from a totally unconscious state of identification with the ego-mind to a higher awareness—we are now aware of the unconsciousness, how it originated, developed and drove our life, creating conflicts and pain. We have become aware of the answers to various fundamental questions of life and also the truth and reality about life. We are clear about the goals to be achieved in life; we know that we need to effect a shift in awareness and bring it to the experiential level, which is the state of awakening. When we consciously reprogramme at the subconscious mind level, we will create new experiences, and new experiences in the brain create new synaptic connections; the neuropeptides associated with new positive emotions send signals to the brain to create similar thoughts, and the new brain circuits are formed and reinforced by repeated similar experiences.[5] So basic awareness about important areas of the brain and their functions will give insight and help the reprogramming process.

In order to become clear about the relevance and importance of reprogramming, let us see a specific nature of the ego-mind. For example, if we had severely felt (or believed to have had) the negative emotion of sense of lack or neglect, or hurt in childhood, this emotion will become a dominant part of the subconscious programme, and it will always manifest through our patterns of thoughts, emotions and behaviour; some may develop a personality trait of seeking more attention and appreciation, or some may become an introvert, so as to avoid such neglect or hurt in future. This programme is played without our awareness, and the ego-mind has the tendency to keep it alive and active so that the negative emotions or reactions are ensured. Now we are aware of the ego-mind's dynamics and the fact that the conclusions made in childhood need not be the truth, it could be wrong conclusions drawn by the child's mind, which ended up becoming the foundation of the programme itself.

We can cherish and undertake a journey to childhood, probably with the help of parents, to revisit some happy memories and also to become aware of the life situations that led to certain conclusions and beliefs, and the subconscious programme itself. One word of caution: some people who have a rigid ego-mind and are stuck in childhood experiences may rekindle negative childhood experiences and react emotionally, which will have undesirable consequences. With higher wisdom, we should be able to revisit our childhood as a 'tourist' without bias or prejudice or judgement, with a smile even in the face of unpleasant experiences. Our purpose is to bring the light of awareness to the dark area and make sense of it. With this mind engineering process, we can bring more awareness to the area of unconsciousness, try to make sense of the childhood life experiences and situations as independent observers, without being sucked into the same emotions or experiences, and we can neutralize the effect and power of this unconscious programme and reprogramme it. Awareness about different parts of the brain and its functions also helps us have higher awareness and facilitate the reprogramming process.

Our childhood emotions and experiences are stored in the limbic brain, which is often referred to as our emotional brain. Our limbic brain is very active, right from childhood, and starts wiring from an early age, as per our experiences. So, we react emotionally to various life situations as we reacted to them in childhood without any awareness.[6] As we perceive everything through sensory signals, the emotional mind or ego-mind interprets and makes sense of various experiences depending upon the subconscious childhood programmes in the limbic brain; thereafter, only the signals are received in the cerebral cortex. So, we emotionally react to signals or life situations rather than responding to them rationally. The perception of reality is likely to have been manipulated at the limbic brain level, which is why different people perceive the same reality in different ways. The intuitive thoughts or feelings and insightful higher awareness are processed in the right hemisphere of the brain. This insight gives us awareness of why we think and feel differently from others and helps us in reprogramming.

The Anatomy between the Two Minds

We have become aware of two non-physical entities: ego-mind and true self. These two entities have, by and large, two distinct processing areas in the brain, the left hemisphere and the right hemisphere. This fact was highlighted by author Arthur Ladbroke Wigan in his theory of 'duality of the mind' back in 1800. Roger W. Sperry highlighted distinct processing areas/ hemispheres of distinct minds in his 1981 Nobel prize lecture: 'The same individual can be observed to employ consistently one or the other of two distinct forms of mental approach and strategy, much like two different people, depending on whether the left or right hemisphere is in use.'[7]

Experience of timelessness or 100 per cent attention to the present moment can be made possible by the right brain. This experience of a higher order of the timeless dimension is the source of real joy or ecstasy. Through the experience of the deeper now, with the right frontal cortex's support, we can experience the interconnectedness with all and everything, perceive all human beings as equals and as parts of the same reality, and feel compassion for fellow human beings.

The left brain provides the linear effect of past and future connection to the present moment experiences to make practical sense of the present, future sequencing and its relevance in the physical world. The ego-mind denies the timeless present moment experiences by relating them to the time dimension, past and future. The left brain is the language processor, and verbalizes the details gathered for communication in practical life. While the right brain perceives events or situations in pictures, the left brain dissects them in different pieces of information and analyses them to make sense.

Incessant thoughts arise in the left brain, and are mainly related to our life in the linear physical world. We are not aware of most of such thoughts, as they emanate from our subconscious mind. Our ego-mind's self-image, including the perception and beliefs of the subconscious mind and the way we react to life events, is based on past experiences and future expectations. Various ego-mind functions—like judgements about things, people or life situations as good or bad and comparisons—are made in the left brain. Our perception of the world as the three-dimensional material world and definition of our own physical boundaries and body consciousness are created by the orientation association areas in the left brain. The right brain processes higher experiences, like feeling our subtle energy body, feeling of bliss or ecstasy, bringing about a sense of everyone being part of one reality, a sense of detachment to worldly things, the experience of everything in the timeless dimension of presence, a sense of wholeness and the self-consciousness as a spiritual being.

The left brain is the source of most of the negative thoughts, negative emotional reactions, addictive and compulsive tendencies, false-negative images and denial of higher positive experiences. It leads to conflict and pain in life, adversely affecting our health and overall wellness.

The right brain perceives and processes longer wavelength signals, giving less importance to the physicality of the material object. It mostly tunes to lower frequencies of sound—subtle body sounds, sounds from nature—facilitating perception of oneness with the nature and the world. The left brain predominantly perceives shorter wavelength and signals from physical surroundings, which promote the perception of the material existence of everything. It usually tunes in to higher frequencies of sound, which are part of our linear material world.

The above awareness gives us clarity about how we think, feel, do or not do something in a particular way. We become aware of the ego-mind's compulsive and addictive patterns to deny us the experiences of the present moment. This higher awareness liberates us from unconscious patterns and gives us an option and power to think, feel and respond to life situations rooted in presence. But, it is a proven fact that by bringing conscious and focussed attention to our thoughts, emotions, higher awareness, spiritual practices, like meditation, and activities anchored in the present moment, higher awareness and resultant experiences can change the wiring pattern of circuits in the left brain and make the right brain stronger and achieve the state of awakening.

The Anatomy of Reprogramming

We know that brain structure or neuronal wirings happen on the basis of our experiences, and once the brain has developed a certain wiring pattern or structure, it will develop a tendency to have similar thoughts, emotions and experiences in the future. So, in order to effect the shift in awareness and transformation, we need changes in the pattern of brain wirings that is possible through new experiences, which in turn are possible with higher awareness and practice of attention in real life. It is also important to become aware of the prime nature of basic brain functioning, its processing and the different aspects of networks facilitating subconscious programmes.

Anatomy of Transformation

We have seen that our subconscious default programme decides our belief system and personality. As a person grows, he becomes ego-conscious, and identifies with the ego-mind and its images and roles. Nature envisages that human beings evolve spiritually along with physical growth. The brainstem grows to its maturity initially, controlling the basic survival functions of the body and then the limbic brain, the emotional brain, and later the neocortex and PFC, which are involved in rational approach and higher awareness. But a person who has developed a dense ego-mind and its rigid identifications is struck at the level of ego-mind consciousness. Once we become aware that we are pure living consciousness and part of cosmic consciousness, our neocortex, PFC and right hemisphere become more active and strong, and our perceptions and belief about everything changes. The consequent signals received by the cells and brains will be then of higher quality; these new experiences will result in new brain structure and transformation of life.

Meditation and the Default Mode Network

The common belief that our brain is rested when we are not doing anything was proved wrong. Scientists identified an area in the brain called default mode network or DMN, which consists mainly of the MPFC, the PCC, which has a direct connection to the limbic system of the brain.[8] When we are focussed on the present moment activity, this default mode is deactivated, only to be activated again when we are not engaged in focussed activities. While we are not engaged in focussed activities in the present moment, our wandering mind is 'hovering' over self-image, desires, needs, past emotional experiences, future anxieties, etc., and also engaged in mind chattering in the form of monologues and dialogues. For a better understanding of the activation of DMN, recall how we often drift away from the meditation process to unwanted thoughts and wandering minds; this is nothing but the DMN in action.

All spiritual traditions followed some form of meditation as a means to get liberation from the addictive and reactive patterns of thoughts, emotions and activities, and access and experience the spiritual dimension of human beings, the awakened state. It should be noted that DMN gets active when stressful tasks are being carried out. Most importantly, it is active when we are worried about what others think, engaged in protecting our ego-image, emotionally reacting as per the subconscious mind programme and feeling anxious about the future. In short, these are basic functions of the ego-mind. On the contrary, it is reported that meditation practices activate prefrontal regulatory circuits, lessen the activities in the DMN, and help us achieve a state of undistracted awareness.[9]

In short, meditation practices enable us to:

i. Observe our own thoughts, emotions and behavioural patterns, and consciously shift our attention to desired activities or thoughts,

ii. Weaken the control of DMN and free us from compulsive and addictive thinking patterns, gaining control over our thoughts and emotions and

iii. Reach a level of manifestation of the higher self and consciousness in the present moment reality

Liberation from Emotional Reaction Pattern Leads to Reprogramming

We have dealt with emotional pain and its various aspects in detail in Chapter 9. As this awareness is critical for transformation and awakening, we should be clear and aware of it at a deeper level to break free from compulsive emotional reaction pattern and reprogramme.

i. **Awareness of its existence:** An open-minded reader should have had this awareness by this time and noticed its pattern in others too. Being aware of its presence within us is the critical state of awareness.
ii. **Awareness of its operation and observation:** We have seen that the ego-mind shows signs of compulsiveness through irritation, uneasiness and uncontrolled negative thoughts or past memories of emotional pain when the ego-mind is craving for emotional pain. A deep awareness of it will help us observe it and defuse its intensity and compulsive nature. This, in turn, will prevent it from creating emotional reactions, conflict and pain in the future.
iii. **Emotional reaction is rooted in the past:** Higher awareness that an emotional reaction pattern is rooted in the past and is relevant and activated only when we perceive the past or future as real, will reduce its intensity and addictive character. When we are aware that the present moment is the only reality, we will gradually free ourselves from the grip of such emotional reactions and unconsciousness.

iv. **We are spiritual beings:** When we are aware and realize that people are spiritual beings, and we do not see others as their ego-images, our perception about others and our pattern of reacting to others will shift, and we will start seeing others as a part of us. This shift in awareness will automatically stop the emotional reaction pattern and conflicts.

Higher Awareness

We have seen that higher awareness is one of the pillars of mind engineering process of reprogramming. A shift in awareness or higher awareness about various aspects of life is a prerequisite for reprogramming the subconscious mind and transformation. Those who have read this book with an open mind have achieved deep awareness of the following basic aspects of life:

i. The ego-mind resists change.
ii. The ego-mind deploys various strategies to resist change and presence.
iii. What should be the goal of life?
iv. We are spiritual beings with human experiences.
v. There are various aspects of the ego-mind dynamics, and that includes identification with the ego-mind.
vi. The experiential aspect of consciousness.
vii. There is an urgent need of practices like meditation.
viii. The present is the only reality.
ix. There is an urgent need for transformation and awakening.

With a shift in awareness through mind engineering wisdom, we can move ahead in the process of subconscious mind reprogramming and achieving a state of awakening, which would liberate us from the control of the ego-mind. As per Vedic wisdom, jnana yoga, the path of knowledge or awareness, is the path of life for realization or awakening.

Awareness and access to the real world

Another aspect of higher awareness is awareness about reality—the real world. When we are identified with our ego-mind, our consciousness is limited to the physical linear world. It implies belief in the time dimension and solidity of matter as reality. Now we are aware that our perception of the material world as reality is an illusion, and everything is energy in different frequencies and vibrations. The belief that we experience the physical world outside of us is also an illusion, as, in reality, all the experiences are processed in the brain and experienced in our mind; in that sense, our brain and mind inside are more real, relevant and important for us than the material world outside. But now we have the higher awareness that we are spiritual beings, consciousness and exist in the timeless dimension. The ultimate goal, as per all spiritual traditions, is to become aware of this truth, and experience it as a human experience in life; in our spiritual journey, we should be able to move from the world of unconsciousness and illusions to the world of reality, i.e., physical realm to mental realm, and then to spiritual realm.

In the normal course, in the process of spiritual development, the physical world and the mental world are relevant as we move ahead through these and deepen the experience of the real spiritual world. When we are identified with the ego-mind, we do not fully experience any of this reality; we live in the illusion of the past or future. The ego-mind exists only in this time dimension, so it denies us the full experience of the physical world as it is in the present through sensory signals. The present sensory signals are also influenced by the past, future and misinterpretations by the ego-mind. So we need to be fully present and experience the presence of the physical world as it 'is', the 'suchness' of the present moment, through sensory signals without prejudicial interpretation of the ego-mind. This is possible when we have the higher awareness. When we are fully experiencing the material world as it is, the mental world comes in alignment; the mind becomes calm and undisturbed by unwanted thoughts and emotions, and its door opens for the deep unbiased experience of the sensory signals. When both these worlds are in alignment, we are automatically closer to the doors of our reality, the beingness.

Reprogramming through Full Attention and Experience

We have seen that we have basically three levels of awareness/reality/worlds which we can experience. The quality of experience of anything depends on the quality of attention we are giving to it. We have been living a life identified with and driven by the ego-mind and experiencing the unreal and illusory past and future. The outcome was worries, conflict, pain and anxiety. As past and future are unreal, their experiences were illusions, and they only helped the ego-mind's purpose of denying the precious presence, the reality. This is the state of unconsciousness, and we have to wake up and realize the truth that we can pay attention to and experience the physical world, mental world and spiritual world only as it is in the now.

We have the higher awareness that the present moment is the reality and does not exist in a continuum. When all three realms (physical, emotional mind and consciousness) fall in alignment, our ego-mind is deactivated.

As higher awareness is the first and foremost pillar of mind engineering wisdom, and being an open-minded and committed reader of the book, you have already become aware of all the wisdom required for awakening; a major shift in awareness has taken place—you are closer to a state of awakening. The following specific methods of reprogramming your subconscious mind will further deepen your experience of higher wisdom, weaken the DMN and strengthen the new brain circuits.

Dialogue with the Ego-Mind

We have seen people engage in authoritative dialogue or debate with others on different topics and situations. Such people do have in-depth knowledge or awareness of the relevant subject or situations. In the context of the mind engineering process, we have become deeply aware of all the aspects of the ego-mind, and with this higher awareness, we can observe all its activities and engage in dialogue with the ego-mind authoritatively. When we become aware of the ego-mind's tendencies to create negative thoughts and emotions without falling prey to its designs, we are then in a position to observe it; we can engage in dialogue with the ego-mind with a smiling face: 'I am aware of the ego-mind designs and you will not succeed in your attempt.' We can now decide what to think, feel, behave and experience. This will break the old ego-mind pattern and the brain will have new experiences. This approach is an effective method to get rid of addiction tendencies. This method is very powerful and effective to weaken the strength of the ego-mind and empower the true self leading to reprogramming and transformation.

Specific Reprogramming Methods

i. **Find the root cause through manifestation:** We know that physical pain is a blessing to diagnose the root cause of illnesses and treating them. Similarly, mental pain or unhealthy emotional or behavioural manifestation can be used as an entry point to access the childhood life situations based on which wrong conclusions were drawn and the subconscious programme was formed. If we cannot be aware of these life situations, the assistance of parents or therapists can be availed to access the root cause, become fully aware of those life situations and make sense of them. This is the methodology of psychoanalysis; once we become aware of the root cause, we can make sense of it without judgement or emotional involvement, and defuse the powerful root or programme that was generating negative thoughts, mental pain, emotional reactions and unhealthy behavioural patterns. This will enable us to gradually come out of its addictive and compulsive patterns, have rational responses, along with new neuronal wirings and brain structures. This will make way for new experiences in the future.

ii. **Repetition of a new programme to rewrite:** Usual wish of the conscious mind to change the subconscious mind patterns will not give any result. Moreover, the subconscious mind will resist any new wisdom that is incompatible with its perceptions and beliefs. So we have to adopt different methods to rewrite the programme, bypassing all these obstructions and resistance. One effective method is repetition of a new programme, ideas or perceptions. When a new idea or programme that our conscious mind wants to achieve is repeated many times for many days, the ego-mind believes it and rewrites the earlier plan. For example, if a low-esteem person repeatedly tells himself, 'I am a confident person' with higher awareness and belief, it will change the subconscious programme. Advertising companies successfully use this method. When we see an advertisement for a product repeatedly for many days, our minds tend to believe its utility, and influence our perception or belief about it. Some scientists suggest practice of 21 days or repetition of 108 times to get the reprogramming done.[10]

iii. **Rewriting the programmes at theta level of the brain:** Our current subconscious mind programme was made in childhood when the brain functioning was at theta level. We have the same theta level brain just before falling asleep or in the initial moments of waking up from sleep. If we reprogramme our minds with new beliefs or ideas just before sleeping and just after waking up, those will superimpose the earlier programmes. For example, a person who is less confident due to conclusions and images of childhood subconscious programme can rewrite it by becoming aware of the childhood situation and making sense of it and imposing new beliefs ('I am a confident person') as the last thoughts before sleep and first thoughts after sleep. Coupled with this practice, awareness of the manifestation of the old programme will reduce its pattern and frequency and facilitate reprogramming.

iv. **Practice mindfulness:** Most of the time, the subconscious programme is active with incessant negative thoughts and mild negative emotions, like irritation, bad mood, low self-esteem, isolation, mild worry, anxiety, etc. When the subconscious mind programme is active, it implies that we are not fully in the present. In order to break this pattern and weaken the corresponding brain circuits, mindfulness should be practised. Though many training programmes are being conducted worldwide on mindfulness, this can be learnt and practised in a simple way very effectively.

Mindfulness means higher awareness of every moment, which is independent of the past and future, and involves giving full attention to the present moment selectively and experiencing it fully. Any subtle or simple activity can give us the experience of presence if we give our full attention to it.

We have seen that about 47 per cent of our activities are routine and mechanical without attention and application of mind. It means that our mind is wandering with negative thoughts related to the past or future, and our 'program' is active during this time and reinforcing it. We can practise mindfulness every moment in every little activity right from the moment we wake up. With insight, we can closely observe our thoughts and emotions. We can be aware of ourselves in waking moments, observe our breathing closely, which itself is meditation, and we can have a positive resolution for the day. We can focus our attention on the body and feel the liveliness of the subtle energy within. We can experience the sensation of the hot or cold water on our face. We can enjoy the gush of the tap water in our washroom. While taking a bath and using soap, visualize and feel that your body is getting a tender whole-body massage. Like this, every subtle activity, which is not usually given attention to, can become means for experiencing the presence. Such mindful practices will deepen and widen the horizon of presence, which was reduced to nil by the ego-mind. This breaks and weakens the pattern of negative thoughts, emotions and behaviour driven by our subconscious mind programme and weakens its brain circuits.

v. **'Yes', the one-word mantra for reprogramming through positivity:** The ego-mind is a negative mind, and about

70 per cent of our daily thoughts are negative. It will have corresponding emotions and behavioural patterns, prompting further negative thoughts, like a vicious circle. This 'program' pattern feeds and strengthens itself and continues till the time we become aware of it. With high awareness of mind engineering wisdom, now we are aware of this pattern. One method of reprogramming can be to bring in positivity by deliberately reciting a very powerful one-word mantra, 'YES', in every situation. When we practice saying 'yes' in every life situation, the old negative pattern is broken, and positive energy is created within the body and around. This pattern will change the neuronal activities, and consequent biochemistry and pave way for reprogramming. It is natural to doubt whether we can say 'yes' to all life situations. How can we agree to a harmful situation? It reminds me of a small incident, when a person asked, 'How can we say "yes" to every situation? Suppose your son asks for one lakh rupees for a party, what will your answer be?' The answer to that would be: 'Yes, my son, let us discuss.' The practice of the 'yes' mantra does not mean that we always agree to all negative situations or behaviour. We can respond rationally in negative situations or in the face of negative behaviours and be assertive that they are not acceptable. 'Yes' means accepting the situation as it is in reality. Resisting reality is negative, and will create conflict and pain. While saying 'yes', we accept the reality, and we respond to it rationally with higher awareness, power and effectiveness. The practice of the 'yes' mantra will change our old programme pattern and help us reprogramme it the way our conscious mind wants.

vi. **Practise blessing others:** When the ego-mind has driven our lives, we always feel a sense of separateness or lack while interacting with others. Our ego-mind always wants to protect its image and position, and relies on conflict and pain for its survival. We have seen that though our conscious mind wants to have peace and harmony in life, we cannot achieve this goal as long as the default programme drives us. Negative thoughts relating to others account for the maximum number of negative thoughts daily. This reinforces our subconscious programme and continues to harm our body, mind and health. Despite having the higher awareness about the ego-mind dynamics, it is not possible to completely stop or be able to regulate negative thoughts overnight. Start blessing others, who come in contact with you either directly or through your memory, with the words 'God bless you'. This will help us reverse the negative thought pattern, which we usually experience on meeting others, into a positive one. Some people find it difficult to sincerely do this, as they might be having an intense difference of opinion with the other person. Being able to do so would mean going against the ego-mind position they were holding on to so far. By now, we have become aware that we all are spiritual beings, part of the same power, like children of the same father or fingers of the same hand. Ill will and conflicts are the language of the ego-mind to create pain in life; it is a toxic substance in our minds that harms only us. When we start meeting others with a blessing for them in our mind, a large number of negative thoughts in a day are discontinued and replaced with very positive thoughts, which will make sudden changes in the brain circuits. This will then reflect in our healing process and overall health and help us in reprogramming.

vii. **Convert ill will to goodwill:** Feeling ill will towards others is one of the most toxic and harmful emotions a human being can have; it is very common and widespread. This emotion has roots in childhood emotions of fear or concern about what others think. It develops to a monstrous level; when we have a dense ego, it manifests in a manner that people with a difference of opinion or rival mental positions are treated as enemies, and an intense ill will is felt and manifested. Such feelings can be observed at every level of society, even in families. The hardened ego-mind has deep-rooted and intense feelings of separateness when interacting with others—this is felt and maintained, complementing the sense of ill will. When this feeling is hardened and manifested, it may develop into a psychic disorder if higher awareness is not brought in and if reprogramming does not take place. Long-term nurturing of ill feeling regarding others has severe consequences on our body and its biochemistry, ultimately resulting in various illnesses. Ill will is like keeping a toxic substance, with harmful radiations, in the head. It harms you primarily, and the harmful radiation indirectly affects your life situations and those of the people around you. We cannot afford to hold on to it even for a moment further if we are aware of its adverse consequences. The decision to convert ill will to goodwill will replace thousands of negative thoughts and emotions with positive counterparts, which will start manifesting with healthy outcomes.

The following higher awareness will help us convert ill will to goodwill:

- As we all are living consciousness, part of one force, any negative thought or ill will against others means it is against ourselves.
- Others will think and feel as per their nature. Bothering about controlling others' thoughts is unconsciousness. When we are a living consciousness, we are whole, as of now, and need not please others.
- Being a powerful living consciousness, we need not seek attention, appreciation or recognition from others.

viii. **Meditation as a tool for reprogramming:** Science has recently acknowledged the multifarious benefits of meditation through various studies. The benefits of meditation are innumerable—it calms down the mind, reduces thoughts and negativity, and helps us experience positive emotions. When positive new experiences are felt, it creates new brain circuits weakening the old pattern and facilitating reprogramming in a sustainable manner. So meditation is the most effective and unique tool for reprogramming our subconscious programme.

13

WHY IS PRACTICE ESSENTIAL?

Once, disciples of a spiritual guru asked, 'Guru, please tell us three things we should do to attain enlightenment.' After a moment of silence, the guru answered, 'Practice,' and remained silent.

The disciples asked, 'What is the next one?'

Guru answered, 'Practice,' and remained silent.

The impatient disciples asked again, 'What is the next one?'

The guru answered, 'Practice.'

Then the disciples understood the importance of practice and that there is no substitute for it.

We have seen that change or transformation is not an easy task, mainly because of the ego-mind's resistance to change. In this modern scientific world, we do not have a dearth of knowledge. It makes sense only if it is applied in practical life. Now, we also have higher wisdom, awareness about subconscious mind reprogramming methods and about the ultimate goal to be achieved. The pre-requirements for achieving this goal are:

i. Taking responsibility for our life,
ii. Commitment to achieving the goals; and
iii. Sincere practice of various methods for reprogramming

When we practice the different methods of reprogramming, we start having new experiences that gradually weaken the brain circuits of the ego-mind and strengthen the circuits supporting our true-self, facilitating sustainable change and transformation. Now, we will see the practical and experiential aspects of the mind engineering process.

Pillars of Mind Engineering

We have seen that three pillars of mind engineering wisdom—higher awareness, 100 per cent attention to reality, and full and deep experience of the presence—facilitate the transformation and leads to the state of awakening. We have also seen that when we are fully present in the physical dimension, mental and spiritual dimensions come in alignment, and the access to and experiences of these realms becomes smooth. This fact has been scientifically validated by a famous study conducted by Dr Alia J. Crum and Ellen J. Langer of Harvard University in 2007.[1] They conducted a detailed study involving 84 female hotel room attendants who were separated in two groups, A and B. Group A was instructed in detail about the surgeon general's recommendations for required daily exercises. They were made aware that their daily work routine is fulfilling these recommendations, and were asked to do these daily activities with awareness and full attention. Group B was not told anything and allowed to continue their routine work as they had been so far. After four weeks, when the parameters of Group A were monitored, the findings were surprising; it was found that they showed marked and substantial improvement in their health parameters compared to the other group. They showed a decrease in weight, blood pressure levels, body fat, waist-to-hip ratio and BMI without making any extra effort. It establishes that when Group A members were trained with higher awareness, trained to give attention to every part of their body and experience the activities in the present fully, their physique transformed in a positive manner, which also enabled them to have a coherent mind.

The Shift from Emotional Reaction to Rational Response

We have seen that when the subconscious mind programmes drive our lives, we follow a pattern of negative emotional reactions. We can rationally respond when we are free from ego-mind's control and pattern, with the true self and rationality driving our life. This shift of awareness and pattern is a prerequisite for our transformation and awakening. All spiritual traditions have conveyed this wisdom in different ways.

Buddha, who lived in the mid-sixth century, taught us that the first noble truth of Buddhism is our basic character of suffering or pain, which is due to:

i. Lack of awareness that everything is impermanent and transitory,
ii. Lack of awareness that all things that arise pass away and
iii. Resistance to reality and obstructing the flow of energy, clinging to the thought forms, i.e., the ego-mind

The second truth is *trishna*, i.e., resistance to change, which means clinging to the ignorance of our subconscious mind or addictive patterns.

The third noble truth can be achieved by transcending the vicious circle of our addictive patterns and freeing ourselves from our bondage of karma or the emotional reaction patterns so that *nirvana* or liberation can be achieved.

Fourth is the eightfold *marga* or the middle path to achieving emptiness or nirvana, which includes higher awareness, meditation, insight, i.e., right seeing and right knowing.

Gita verses 4.42 give a clear idea about adopting a rational approach in life instead of an emotional one. Lord Krishna said, 'Kill, therefore, with the sword of wisdom, the doubt born of ignorance that lies in the heart. Be one in self-harmony, in Yoga, and arise, great warrior, arise.' We should know that the ego-mind is our greatest enemy, and we have to wake up, arise as warriors with the sword of wisdom to respond rationally.

When we are unconscious and identified with the ego-mind, we follow a negative emotional reaction pattern, which is not as required and justified in different life situations. Most of the time, the reactions at our emotional and behavioral levels are either 'more' or 'less' than the required action. Now we are aware of the emotional reactions and stress that we have been experiencing in different degrees, especially in life situations involving interaction with others and their impact on our health and wellness. Practising the principle 'nothing more, nothing less' is a very effective method to face difficult life situations and remain calm, relaxed and happy. This is rationality in action. This can be a frequent mental exercise; after facing any life situation or interaction with people, we can introspect and assess whether we followed this rule or not; we can evaluate our body language, tone, actions and expressions. We should minutely review what was our state of mind while interacting with others, whether we were maintaining our cool and rationality or whether we were emotionally excited or low or stressed. This awareness or insight about our state of mind and ability to observe it will help us control and regulate it gradually. This will also help develop rational response patterns and a better personality. Now being aware of it and having the insight, we can effect a shift in our approach to life, from an emotional reaction to a rational response in every life situation. We will think, feel and act only as justified and required in a given situation, nothing more, nothing less. This approach is going to make a huge difference in all aspects of life.

How Rigid Ego-Mind Creates Conflict and Pain?

What do we call a person if he is deliberately choosing unhappiness and pain in life? What do we call a person who is holding a hot coal, despite suffering burns and pain? Unconscious, fool or insane? We can understand if he is completely unconscious or insane. If he is not and still causing hurt to himself knowingly then unconscious or foolishness would be mild words for him. Are we not doing the same thing if we go on creating conflict and pain despite attaining mind engineering wisdom?

So far, we were not aware of the dynamics of the ego-mind, its strategies and that about 70–80 per cent of our thoughts are negative and repetitive, leading to negative emotions and lifestyles. We were not aware of its basic nature of creating conflict and pain. We were not aware that we are fully identified with our ego-mind, and this unconsciousness caused us to live in the negative zone, a situation similar to this unconscious person holding a hot coal and creating pain for himself. But when he becomes aware of it, he will definitely drop it and put an end to his sufferings. But what about us? We were also doing the same thing so far. Instead of hot coal, we were keeping 'imaginary problems', which are either wrong interpretations of the ego-mind or related to the past or future, which are all unreal and do not exist. The present moment is the only reality. If the present moment is an unfavourable situation, either avoid it or modify it; if not possible, face it rationally. Now that you are aware of it, are you willing and ready to put an end to creating conflict and pain in life? You are aware that now you have an option to drop it or hold on to it; if you drop it, you can have lots of good fortunes and can have a fulfilling life.

Dense ego-mind may cause psychic disorders

Certain extreme forms of ego-mind patterns and manifestations of rigid ego-mind may develop into personality or mental disorders or illnesses. As all of us are driven by the ego-mind, ego-driven negative thoughts, emotions and behavioural patterns are considered normal and normal life goes on unabatedly. Though the sufferers are not aware of it, others can sense these abnormal behavioural patterns. People who have had bitter childhood experiences, like severe hurt, neglect, abuse and torture, unless made aware of it, may develop rigid ego-mind manifestations, like trying to project the ego-mind image, the personality trait of introversion, violent nature, behavioural disorders, paranoias, like persecution mania, fearing conspiracies or plots by others, etc. The mind engineering wisdom, practices and meditation can transform them, bringing in higher awareness, new positive and healthy patterns in their life.

Work life and ego-mind

Most of us have a structured work life in which we spend the major portion of our lives and interact with many people formally. In formal life situations, the conscious mind becomes stronger and takes control to some extent, and it usually does not allow the ego-mind to manifest the patterns of the subconscious mind outwardly. The ego-mind creates a camouflage and tries to create artificially looking normal life situations. It creates a situation of unmanifested conflict between the subconscious mind and conscious mind. Some of us cannot always control the subconscious mind programme, and it is manifested during unfavourable situations in the form of conflict and stress in the workplace. When the ego-mind is active at work, it affects efficiency, and it pops up thoughts and emotions involving 'I', 'me', 'mine', 'you' and 'yours' related to work and the people involved; it leads to poor quality of work, causing conflict, pain and stress. When there is a colleague with a dense ego-mind, it will also trigger others' ego-minds, and resultant emotional reactions will vitiate the workplace's conducive atmosphere. When the ego-mind is a dominant factor in the workplace, it will also adversely affect the quality of work, merit and capabilities of others at work and the overall efficiency of the organization.

But there are many people with strong conscious minds, rationality and higher virtues who work passionately in their respective places with complete focus, involvement and abilities, finding meaning, satisfaction and fulfilment in their jobs. The mind and body of such people are in the positive zone and a healthy state. Those who take work as a spiritual experience are the blessed ones in their professional life.

Sensory Perceptions Can Deepen the Presence

We can hear a sound when there is a background of silence or space. This silence or space in which the sound exists allows us to experience that sound. When we can listen to a sound in this dimension with the awareness of the background silence, the quality of listening is at the highest level, and more than listening, it is an experience of the whole body and mind in the present—a spiritual experience. Similarly, all sensory perceptions can become spiritual experiences, and our life can become a manifestation of our spiritual essence through human experiences.

Immunity the Ego-Mind's Provocations and Conflicts

We have seen that negative thoughts, emotions, suffering and problems adversely affect our quality of life. The transformation process through mind engineering will enable us to face such life situations rationally without mental pain, problems and stress. We have become aware of how the ego-mind originates, develops, operates and drives our lives. If this awareness is deeply registered as wisdom, a shift in perception has taken place, and we will become immune to egoic patterns and not get provoked by unfavourable life situations or others' ego-minds.

The Need of Mind Engineering Wisdom

We have seen the dynamics of the ego-mind at the individual level in depth, so we can stop identifying with it, reduce its control on us, bring in higher wisdom and quicken the process of transformation. While interacting with specific groups, the ego-mind becomes part of a collective ego-mind identity, which becomes a great force in society. Such collective ego-mind functions as collective unconsciousness, which leads to a lot of conflicts between groups in society. We have seen that though our civilization has excelled in the field of science and technology, and many of us have a lot of fortunes in life, we find lots of conflicts at the individual and collective levels. On the other hand, spiritual wisdom is spreading as never before as a last resort for finding peace, joy and wellness in life as modern science has its limitations when it comes to finding true happiness in life.

The Need of Mind Engineering Training

Mind engineering wisdom is essential to be imparted to and imbibed by everyone to break free from the control of the ego-mind, rise to one's full potential and have a fulfilling life. But the following critical groups in society are more vulnerable or have a significant influence on others, or the nation at large, which is why the need of mind engineering training for them increases.

Children: Children are the hope of the present generation. As the subconscious mind programme is the foundation of their personality, children need to be imparted with positive experiences or 'strokes' by the caregivers to enable them to have a healthy programme, which would facilitate them in learning how to approach different life situations rationally.

People with predominantly technical brains: Most of the qualified human resources, especially professionals, predominantly use their left brain, which supports technical and logical thinking. So their left brain becomes stronger and supports the ego-mind and its tendencies. Such people tend to be more emotional and stressed in different life situations, thereby, in need of mind engineering training.

Teachers and parents: They are the main programmers of children's personalities, so they should be well aware of this wisdom. They should be well aware of their approach and interactions with the children, as the latter draw conclusions from every minute of their interactions.

Decision-makers or policymakers: The decisions made by people who run the government or organizations or corporates have far-reaching consequences in society, affecting wellness and welfare of a large population and even future generations. It is necessary for them to have a rational mind and approach, along with a broader perspective, which is possible when they are free from the control of their ego-mind. Unfortunately, many such people make decisions prompted by the ego-mind, with a narrow vision, adversely affecting organizations and society.

Religious leaders: Religion plays a vital role in society and has a great influence on people in many ways. So the religious leaders can bring about positive changes within communities if they preach and practise the true spirit of religious teachings or the true spiritual wisdom, like what mind engineering offers.

Structured organizations: State of mind, attitude, nature of perception of human resources of all structured organizations significantly influence the efficiency and success of such bodies. So imparting training of mind engineering wisdom will help enhance the efficiency and effectiveness of the workforce at such organizations.

People who need a specific performance, like students or sportspeople: Mind is a critical aspect of performance in any field, especially where individual performance is involved, like sports and games. Usually, people facing such situations are emotional in nature, and they cannot bring out their full potential during their game, which affects their performance level. Mind engineering training will help them tide over such issues and help them focus on their performance with full potential and achieve success.

Mind Engineering Tips for Stress Management

Stress is the primary offshoot of the ego-mind-driven life, which has many adverse consequences on health and overall wellness. Nowadays, everybody, especially the executives working in senior positions and the corporate world, are reeling under severe stress. Many people have achieved a lot in life but suffer from different types of mental pain due to stress. Achievements would hold no significance when there is no peace of mind and happiness in life. Stress means the absence of mental peace and happiness. A higher level of education or position does not help; medical science has concluded that most illnesses are results of mental stress. Simultaneously, everyone has a deep urge to achieve peace, happiness and good health in life. To achieve this goal, most of us resort to activities like exercises, yoga, pranayama, seeking the guidance of gurus, reading self-help books, visiting religious places, observing penance, and the list goes on. Many people are willing to spend large amounts of money or time to achieve this goal of a stress-free life with peace of mind and happiness. What should be done? Let us have a closer look.

When we were children, we all led a stress-free, healthy, peaceful, playful life without worries of the past, without anxieties of the future, with our basic needs being attended to. Let us see how did we complicate our lives as we grew up. Let us understand what stress is all about. Stress is a negative and harmful mental state, which arises due to our inability to cope with a situation; it is the gap between the present and the expected situation. So, the problem is our expectations, which most of us are not aware of. It shows that our mind has a strong expectation from every situation. In other words, stress is due to resistance or non-acceptance of the situation, which we do not like. But the given situation is reality; resisting or non-acceptance of reality is nothing but unconsciousness or foolishness on our part.

We know the options: if the unfavourable situation can be avoided, do so, if not, the only option available is to modify it to suit us. If neither is doable, accept it with grace and face it rationally. This higher awareness will help us face situations rationally without creating stress. Let us see some examples. An executive may say that stress is due to work pressure or X assignment. We always attribute the reason for stress to a particular situation. Is it right? Most of us think it is correct, but the truth is that attributing reason to stress is wrong. Of course, one should have enough technical capability to do the tasks assigned, and if required, get the necessary training. Let us understand the truth closely. Given the same capabilities, will all the executives having the same assignment have the same stress level? The answer is no; the stress level varies among them despite being in the same situation. Now, we become aware of the truth that stress is not due to any reason or situation but because of our nature. The same situation may be stressful for one, but not for another. This fundamental awareness is the basic awareness we should have to come out of stress in life.

Now, what is our nature? Our nature depends on our perceptions. Our perceptions are developed from the way we interpret life situations from our childhood onwards. In the absence of proper awareness, we learnt to perceive different life situations as threatening and faced them with emotional reactions like fear, anxiety and stress. This sum total of perceptions becomes a major portion of our subconscious programme or personality manifesting in the form of worries of the past and anxieties of the future. So, stressful patterns of life become a routine experience.

This, again, is due to the absence of proper awareness. We are not stressed about the present moment or situation, which is the only reality. Worry or stress is based on past experience or future anxiety. With a higher level of awareness, we are aware that the past and future are unreal. The only option available is to do whatever best is possible now, with a rational plan for the future. Our emotional reaction to something not existing and unreal—past and future—is only creating stress, which is nothing but again unconsciousness or foolishness. The reality is only the present.

Of course, we can use the past information for enriching the present and future planning. What is real is the present moment; we can only do whatever is best possible in the present. Thinking about the past and the future will lead to stress, and that will reduce our ability to give our best in the present. In short, we are creating stress in our life due to unconsciousness or lack of proper awareness. Everybody has the birthright to lead a stress-free and happy life. What happened when we grew up? We complicated life with wrong perceptions, gradually lost our natural qualities and developed a false image and perceptions, blocking our original positive qualities. With higher levels of awareness, we can change our perceptions, resulting in positive experiences, which can then effect changes in the brain. This will pave the way for positive and permanent transformation. In short, we create stress and related problems when we consider the unfavourable life situation as a threat which has debilitating effect on our potentials. When we consider such situations as challenges following a rational approach, it enhances our potentials to face unfavourable life situations. This will help us lead a happy, peaceful and stress-free life.

Contentment: A State of Awakening

A sense of lack is the nature of the ego-mind, and a state of full contentment is the nature of consciousness or state of awakening. It means that a person driven by the ego-mind is never fully satisfied, and he believes that he will be happy, satisfied and fully contented only with the fulfilment of certain conditions in future, which might never happen. As long as the ego-mind drives us, we will have this approach. Moreover, once one condition is fulfilled, another one pops up, and the cycle goes on. We have seen that we can be contented only in the now, and that experience is denied by our ego-mind.

Let us look at it more closely. When an animal is sated and is present in a specific natural habitat, it is fully contented. A child is fully contented with basic natural requirements, like sufficient food, care, etc. When we grow up, and when we identify with our ego-mind/image, our needs become unlimited and never-ending due to its sense of lack. There is no point in time when we are fully contented. A multibillionaire is taking a lot of trouble and stress, sacrificing his health and wellness to earn more, and a slight loss in one year will give him nightmares. Why? Some may argue that if people remain idle being fully content, there will not be any development in the world. No. What we are examining here is the state of our mind. A person who has reached a state of contentment can focus more energy and put in more efforts effectively and rationally on his activities or endeavours.

Another question people ask is, 'How can we feel contented when there are unfavourable situations or problems like illnesses?' We have seen that it is natural to have unfavourable life situations. If unavoidable, we have to face these realities rationally. We are talking about the state of mind and sense of lack that drives us and keeps us unsatisfied all the time in life, even when many of us have a lot of fortunes in life.

Ultimately, our goal is to have a better quality of life. Our quality of life depends on our quality of experiences in life, which rests in the present. If fortunes of life do not help us enhance the quality of our experiences, they hold no value then. Similarly, our higher awareness and wisdom should be experienced and manifested in real life. So let us delve into the experiential aspect of our higher awareness and wisdom.

14

ACCESSING AND EXPERIENCING AWAKENING

When we are not living our life in the present, we are living in a state of unconsciousness. It is essential to have full awareness about this state of unconsciousness, its depth and intensity, as that will help us come out from not being present and commit ourselves to undertaking the transformation and awakening process.

We will try to understand this with the help of a few examples. Visualize a few simple situations: 1. a student is not paying attention to his studies at all, instead he is more interested in unwanted activities, 2. a person is eating delicious food while talking on mobile phone all throughout, and 3. instead of giving attention to his family or spouse, a person is more concerned about the affairs of others in his vicinity. In all these examples, the people involved are not paying attention to and doing justice to their roles. What do we call them? Unconscious? Irresponsible? Or all of the above?

Now, let us look at ourselves—we, too, are not aware of or pay attention to our thoughts, emotions and behavioural patterns. We always focus our attention on illusory past and future by way of emotional reactions. We are mostly bothered about what others think, feel and do, creating pain and conflicts. When we are not paying attention to our life, which is in the present, most of the time, what should we call ourselves then?

Most of us are not aware of the precious gift we lost as we gradually grew up. As a child, we had the ability to be aware of the 'isness' or 'suchness' of the present moment, pay full attention to it and deeply experience it. If a child looks at an interesting thing, like a fish, or if he is engaged in an interesting activity or game, he pays full attention to it, deeply experiencing it, not letting it get influenced by the past or future; he forgets about every other thing in the world around him. This precious faculty of children is the foundation of future spiritual development, a life rooted in the present moment reality. But as and when our ego-mind developed and gradually strengthened based on past experiences, it developed an illusion that its needs and desires can be fulfilled only in the future. We started perceiving the world and life situations relating them to the past and future in a linear manner, i.e., the past-present-future continuum. Gradually, past and future received more illusory attention, and experience of the present became reduced to practically nil. The ego-mind gradually developed this deep unconsciousness, and almost all thoughts, emotions and actions became related to the past and future. We developed a pattern of emotionally reacting to past and future (mostly immediate past and immediate future); the ego-mind ensured that we are denied the present and the experience of reality.

We have to regain the paradise lost; the readers of this book have a good opportunity. We need to be fully responsible and committed in bringing this wisdom to reality in life. Now our goal is clear and accessible at arm's length. We have to perceive the world and life situations as they are in the present and respond rationally to them, with limited relevance to the past and future. We have to bring full awareness to ourselves, the physical, mental and spiritual aspects every day, right from the moment we open our eyes in the morning. We should be aware of every subtle movement of our body and activity, pay full attention to it, such that every activity becomes an experience in itself. At the mind level, we should be aware of the coming thoughts, our state of mind and emotions, which we usually never pay attention to. This is a powerful practice that will help us avoid unwanted negative thoughts and emotions of the ego-mind and anchor ourselves in the present with positive thoughts and feelings. When we are able to bring full awareness and attention to the present moment and deeply experience it, we reach the threshold of awakening.

Now being aware of this deep state of unconsciousness, we should bring higher awareness into our lives through the process of mind engineering. Now we have the insight and awareness about who we are. We have to bring in consciousness or awareness at the experiential level of our lives, which means the present. We should be aware of all our activities, including very little and subtle ones, and state of being in the physical and mental aspects in the present moment. At the physical level, we have five active senses and their experiences; at the mind level, we have thoughts, emotions and various subjective experiences. Every little sensory experience, like listening to a bird's song, seeing an object, tasting a dish, smelling a fragrant flower can be a thrilling experience when we are fully in the present. Similarly, awareness about the emotions being manifested on our faces helps us become aware of the nature of thoughts and emotions in mind, which is a very powerful practice for regulating thoughts and emotions. If we closely observe and become aware of our patterns of doing things, we will realize that most of them are automatic and learnt patterns. When we are fully aware of all these, we will be able to pay full attention to them, and experience them fully in the present—this will be the state of awakening.

We have become fully aware that we are spiritual beings, pure living consciousness, with human experiences. When we are leading a life driven by consciousness, our basic approach becomes rational in all life situations (instead of the emotional approach of the ego-mind). With the mind engineering process and practices, we could transform from the negative zone to the positive zone (consciousness-driven rational life). The extent of transformation depends on our effectiveness in addressing ego-mind's resistance to change, open-mindedness and commitment to transformation. Some people who feel that they cannot transform substantially should become aware of this and commit themselves to undergo the process after addressing the ego-mind's resistance to change.

In ancient times, people were more concerned with body consciousness and their physical survival. In the twenty-first century, the world's scenario has changed, and most of us do not have to face survival issues, like the danger of being attacked by a wild animal. We have made a lot of advancements in the field of science and technology, which have given us physical comforts. People have become more logical and technical in the way they think. They have developed an addiction to the linear material world. These developments have hardened our ego-mind, causing our spiritual development to get eroded. Stress, suffering and pain have increased like wildfire with resultant health and wellness problems. People have started looking for a means of mental peace and happiness. Many of them have started realizing the real path for finding solutions to it, i.e., the path of spiritual awakening.

Though the core teachings of all spiritual wisdom and traditions involve bringing about a shift in awareness and freeing us from the control of the ego-mind, leading to awakening, the ego-mind successfully resisted these by misinterpreting the teachings and denying us the experience of the present moment through its various strategies. Another reason why various precious spiritual teachings could not result in the intended effect is the underestimation of the strength of the ego-mind to resist change or to resist a shift in awareness. The ego-mind is very strong and the resistance wall of the ego-mind against new wisdom or shift in awareness is not easily breakable. When we are unconscious, all our resources and intelligence are at the ego-mind's command; it uses all our intelligence to find excuses or justifications, to not accept new awareness and deny full attention and experience of higher wisdom, the experience of the present moment.

Some scientists are of the view that the processing area of the ego-mind has one million times more processing capacity compared to the processing area of our true self.[1] The best strategy to face a strong enemy is to become fully aware of its strength, all its strategies and the way it operates. Higher awareness about the enemy will weaken him (ego-mind), and we will gain strength at a much higher level. Unlike other wisdom, the mind engineering process fully exposes the ego-mind, makes us aware of its origin, development, operations and enables us to become aware of the various strategies and illusions it adopts in detail. This empowers us to liberate ourselves from the control of the ego-mind and attain the goal of awakening.

We Are More Powerful Than We Think

As the ego-mind is our enemy, it always wants to create a poor and negative image of us with primordial negative emotion of fear. The ego-mind wants us to live with this emotion in different degrees and manners, sometimes hidden in mild form and sometimes manifested severely, depending on the interpretation and perception of the life situations. Once we start carrying this basic emotion in us, every action and life itself becomes of poor quality. We have seen that fear originates from the threat to physical existence experienced right from birth, which is a defense mechanism deep-rooted in our minds. When we develop an ego-mind identity, the threat to ego-mind image is experienced in the same brain circuits, sometimes more severely. In short, fear has become an inseparable part of our ego-mind identity.

The ego-mind creates a poor image of us in respect of our capabilities and potentials. At the physical level, we have much greater capabilities than we believe. Look at the various sports personalities; they were born as ordinary human beings. It was after training and practice that they started showing better physical abilities compared to others. We can even keep the examples of sportspeople aside. A 15-year-old girl Jyoti Kumari, hailing from a poor family, from a village in Sikenderpur, Haryana, cycled to Darbhanga, Bihar, with her aged father sitting pillion for 1,200 km in eight days during the Covid-19 lockdown.[2] It was reported that in April 2013, two teen-aged girls, Hannath Smith (16) and her sister Haylee (14), in Lebanon, lifted a 3000-pound tractor to free their father from under it.[3] Well-trained Shaolin monks, too, display an unimaginable level of physical endurance and literally superhuman physical abilities.

We do have an amazing level of mental strength. There are thousands of cases of incurable diseases, like cancer, getting healed with the power of the mind. Studies have found that energy healing is a reality, and the energy from the healer is transmitted to the targeted person.[4] Buddhist meditators can live freezing temperatures in the Himalayas without any protection, adjusting their body temperature with the power of their mind. Zen practitioners control many body functions, including blood flow from a cut in the body, using the power of the mind. There are many reports of skin diseases having healed through hypnotic suggestions. It is proved that we can create our own reality in life with the right. Studies have also reported cases of remote viewing and moving objects with the power of the mind.[5]

Now, we are aware that we are spiritual beings, consciousness, with human experiences, and many of our abilities are limited or constricted by our perceptions or beliefs of our ego-mind. Once we have this wisdom at the experiential level, we will be able to come out of the poor image created by the ego-mind. If this wisdom is imparted systematically and scientifically as a structured training programme, we can enable people to unleash their unlimited potentials and performance in different functional areas, like improved efficiency on the work front, performance in sports, etc. We have seen many awakened people who have been able to lead blissful lives, and have become world spiritual leaders and sources of motivation to many across the world. Many of them were ordinary people in the earlier half of their life. Some were even introverts with low self-esteem, but went on to become world spiritual leaders after reaching the state of awakening. There are many cases of people who experienced consciousness through NDE/OBE and have achieved higher spiritual wisdom. They have healed their incurable illnesses, manifested many higher abilities and have become ambassadors of this higher wisdom to a larger population across the world.

In a way, we all are 'supermen' with a lot of unmanifested potential and abilities, which are inhibited by our perceptions, beliefs and the image created by our ego-mind and collective ego-minds of various organizations and ideologies to which we belong. Though we are fully aware that we are powerful and spiritual beings with immense potential to experience and manifest it, we have to be free from the control of the ego-mind and have to effect changes in the pattern of brain circuits that support ego-mind patterns. As we know that new experiences will change the wiring pattern of brain circuits, we need to reinforce the new wisdom and awareness, reprogramme the subconscious mind, practise the suggested methods and experience them in daily life.

When we free ourselves from the control of the ego-mind through the mind engineering process, we become free from the subconscious programme or 'autopilot' and its basic nature like fear, conflict, sense of lack and separateness; we can unleash our unlimited potentialities. For example, when we have the higher wisdom at the experiential level that we are spiritual beings or living consciousness, which is immortal, we become free from fear of death; once we are free from fear of death, we are free from all types of fears. Such a fearless person feels very powerful physically, mentally and spiritually. Such spiritually awakened people will manifest the nature of true self, i.e., love, peace, joy, compassion and rationality in daily life.

Like a hard shell within which we live, identification with the ego-mind image is very strong, and higher awareness and practices are required to come out of it. Many groups, of which we are a part of, are collective manifestations of the ego-minds of the people. There are many organizations and ideologies carrying out the agenda of the ego-mind in a collective manner. People are made slaves of such organizations and ideologies; they identify with such organizations, ideologies, their practices and rituals, and live like their slaves without any room for independent thinking and free will. They are made to believe that their life purposes, goals and fulfilment will be possible only through such organizations and ideologies, without being aware of the truth. The core teaching of all spiritual wisdom aims at liberating us from such bondage and enabling us to lead a life of free will and rationality, manifesting higher potential and consciousness.

Many instances are mentioned in the various religious texts about the manifestation of superhuman spiritual abilities by different personalities. Famous Arabic folk stories of 'fisherman and the genie' and 'Aladdin and the magic lamp' also indicate the magnificent spiritual powers of human beings, which are contained and restricted in the bottle or the lamp (the ego-mind) without being able to manifest through free will.

Our potential consciousness is also contained within us and restricted by our ego-mind. I believe such stories are intended to make us aware and realize that we are powerful spiritual beings contained in the body and restricted by our ego-mind. In order to be in touch with your consciousness, you can practice meditation right before you sleep—close your eyes, and experience the liveliness of your consciousness with all its qualities and nature; take a deep breath observing the flow of the breath and visualize that your consciousness is emerging out of the body, like in the story of the 'genie', and observe your healthy body from above, feeling the nature of consciousness—deep love, peace, joy and unlimited potentials. Visualize and feel that you are powerful. Recall instances of the emotional reactions you had in the day and realize that you could rationally respond to it without creating conflicts and do so in future events too, making resolutions about life the way you want. This practice will help you bring a deeper awareness of consciousness at an experiential level. Being part of a larger consciousness or divinity, you have unlimited potential and capabilities, which are limited by the body and ego-mind consciousness. Once this wisdom is deeply registered at the subconscious level, the blockade of ego-mind will disappear, and consciousness and your higher potentialities will emerge, like the shining sun emerging from behind the thick clouds.

To put it in another example, suppose a beggar, who has wandered the streets since his childhood without knowing about his kin, was identified as a family member of a powerful kingdom based on the ring he was wearing; visualize how morally elevated and powerful he would feel. After that, suppose it was found out that he was a lost child from the royal family itself!

How much more powerful would we feel when we realize that we are not the ego-mind but a spiritual being or consciousness and part of the all-powerful divinity or the Almighty? Remember, you do not belong to this larger consciousness; much more than that, you are part of it, as in the case of the prince. Do you need to be bothered about what others think? Do you want to please others and seek their attention and appreciation?

Spiritual Development, the Need of the Hour

Ancient man lived in harmony with nature, and nature provided everything for his survival, health and wellness. Man was predominantly body-conscious. In the history of the evolution of humanity, along with the material world, man developed identification with things—material and non-material—and created an image out of it, which is the ego-mind. It includes material possessions, names, forms, patterns of thought, emotions, behaviour and the ego-mind image—predominantly ego-mind consciousness. When the whole civilization is ego-mind conscious and materialistic, conflicts and pain are common features everywhere. Nature envisages human beings to evolve spiritually, as we are spiritual beings in essence. When we evolve spiritually, a new dimension will emerge in everything.

We have seen that materiality or solidity is an illusion, and everything is energy in different vibrations and frequencies. Everything exists in the background of the spiritual realm or space. When we perceive everything in the spiritual realm, it adds a spiritual dimension and depth to every experience; the quality of our perception multiplies when we experience it to its fullest in the present. This dimension emerges when we segregate things from the materialistic linear world by creating space for everything. When we experience everything through our sensory perception in this dimension, we experience the manifestation of liveliness in everything.

But is this a more congenial time for spiritual awakening? The answer is yes and no. No, because more and more people are getting deeply engaged with the time dimension, linear ego-mind world and its experiences, and corresponding brain networks are getting hardened. Many of them take the support of materialistic or reductionist scientific approaches to stick to their mental positions.

Yes, because of the ego-mind-driven life pattern, despite the presence of many physical amenities in life, suffering, stress, conflicts and pain of common man are increasing day by day, and many are feeling the urge from deep within to change or transform to have joy, peace, health and wellness in life. Different new branches of science, like quantum mechanics, recognize that everything is energy and consciousness is the fundamental force of the universe. Many scientific studies, like the one conducted by Southampton University in 2014, have proved that human consciousness exists beyond the death of a person and human beings are spiritual beings with human experience. About 50 years of research by Virginia University has come out with many undeniable pieces of evidence about rebirth or reincarnation. Many instances of NDEs, especially

NDEs of people blind by birth and their narration of their visual experiences during OBE, are undeniable evidence that we are spiritual beings. There are many developments and testimonies, like the healing of incurable diseases with the power of the mind and innumerable health and wellness benefits of meditation, that medical science cannot provide. Living examples of enlightened people and testimonies of many famous scientists and their experiences are the real motivation for many open-minded people to undertake the journey towards spiritual awakening. Yes, the time is riper than ever. It is an urgent need and a medical emergency.

Awakened human experience

Spiritual development does not mean that the material world and things are irrelevant. With higher awareness, we can enjoy human experiences of the material world. Our quality of actions and experiences of material things will be of a higher order then. Non-possession of things, names or forms will not reduce our identity, beingness, or who we are. Life will be a free flow.

Awakened life in the material world will have the following experiential aspects:

i. **Harmony and cordiality in interactions:** We have seen that in an egoic world, conflict with other people, whether mild or severe, is frequent everyday, which creates stress and pain with a lot of adverse consequences in life. This happens due to basic unconsciousness about us and others; now, when we are aware that we all are spiritual beings and part of the same entity, there is no room for conflicts. Though others will continue to interact from a state of identification with the ego-mind, we will not emotionally react to such situations and rationally respond without being taken over by our ego-mind. We will not judge a person based on their ego-mind patterns. Such a response or pattern will also bring in more sanity and awareness in others. When a person is holding a lit candle in darkness, others around also benefit from the light.

ii. **Aware of the illusion:** Now we will be fully aware of the illusion of the past-present-future continuum and aware that the present is the only reality that exists in isolation in which we ever live; this is the entry point to the experience of our beingness and state of awakening. With a deep awareness of this truth and a deeper experience of the present, we can widen the horizon of the 'now' and live a life rooted in the state of awakening.

iii. **Acceptance of the reality:** A lifestyle and approach with 'yes' to all life situations means a sense of acceptance of every moment, which is the opposite of egoic resistance or emotional reaction to reality. This will help us bring rationality to all life situations, actions and responses, which will be of high quality and order.

iv. **Higher awareness:** Now, we have higher spiritual wisdom and a shift in awareness has taken place—we will perceive everything in the spiritual dimension. We are aware that we all are part of the same force and deeply connected. Our basic nature is love and compassion. When we do and experience everything in this higher awareness, our life in the material world becomes more enriched and meaningful.

v. **Pleasant experience and enthusiasm:** We will perform all actions with enthusiasm, and all actions will give us joy, a pleasant experience and a sense of fulfilment. Every cell in the body will be involved in all actions and experiences in a healthy and pleasant manner. Every little activity will be a spiritual experience. We can find some examples of people doing different activities as spiritual experiences—a loving mother taking care of her child, a passionate sportsperson practising his game—all these activities are performed with higher awareness, full attention and experience in the present.

Experience of the State of Awakening

Awakening is a state of deep and higher awareness and experience about oneself, others and the world. It will result in a shift in awareness, experience, altered consciousness, emotion and behavioural patterns with a rational approach manifesting our beingness or consciousness anchored fully in the present moment; our body and mind will manifest it as higher potential, good health and wellness in life.

Some may have apprehension, after reading the book, whether they are awakened or not. There is no common yes or no answer for this. The relevant question you should ask yourself is: 'How far I am awakened?' It depends on how far you have been open-minded, receptive and committed without the resistance of the mind. Every reader will experience some extent of awakening. Most of the readers will have gone through the book because of their commitment, open-mindedness and readiness to be awake; for them, a great extent of awakening has taken place, and many may not be aware of it as there is no immediate physical manifestation. This is not like someone going to the gym, with the results getting reflected in their physique. This internal qualitative change will show in your body by way of more energy, immunity, healing, grace on your face, good health; you will feel at peace, and have love, joy and compassion in your mind. Your daily activities will be of higher quality, as you will be free of problems, stress and conflicts. Your activities will bring about a pleasant experience, manifesting your higher self, which will also positively affect the people around you—be it in family or workplace. They will notice the changes and tell you about them.

Every step of awareness (each chapter) helps us dig deeper into the process of awakening. Every step of awareness is like lighting a candle in a large area of darkness, but we know that even a small lit candle can make a huge impact in a pitch-dark area. Now we decide what to think, feel and do in our life. We are no more a slave of the ego-mind, but do not underestimate it. It will try to gain strength with new strategies and games. So we should stay vigilant and deepen our awareness level and awakening by practising meditation, yoga, pranayama, bringing in more and more awareness to every little activity, staying more in the present moment. If you were an open-minded and committed reader, you are a different person by now.

With higher mind engineering wisdom, we are well aware of the unconscious life we have led so far in the material world in the time dimension, illusory past and future; most of the time in life was wasted bothering about what others think and so on. We now decide to put a full stop to this unconsciousness; we decide to live only in reality, present and not in illusions (past and future). We know three worlds or realms of reality, i.e., the physical world, mental world and spiritual world. When we remain fully present in the physical realm through full attention and experience of this primary reality, other realms will fall in alignment. Now we are aware of the present moment, the physical realm as it 'is' now, and we decide to focus only on reality from now onwards. As the ego-mind will tend to distract our attention, we should ask ourselves as frequently as we can, 'Where is my attention,' and that will help us bring back our attention to the present if it had drifted to the past or future and refocus on the present reality and experience with a 100 per cent with insight and awakening.

Awakening is not something to be understood through literal meaning or with an analytical mind. It is a shift in our awareness at the subconscious mind level and experience, which means at the level of perceptions and beliefs. It will manifest in real life through changes in thoughts, emotions, experiences and behavioural patterns. When we undertake the inner journey of mind engineering towards awakening, it does not mean that we reach a particular point of time of awakening at the end of the journey. At each level of higher awareness or wisdom, we are deepening the awakening process. So, the extent of awakening will vary from reader to reader. You need not look for symbols of awakening taking place; your own changes in the way you think, feel, behave, the experience of joy, peace, good health and wellness are the symbols.

Introspection

With higher awareness and a 100 per cent attention to and experience of the present moment and activities, we have reached a state of awakening. Some readers may feel that they have reached awakening to a limited extent only; they need to reinforce and deepen their higher awareness and practice various reprogramming methods we have addressed earlier without allowing the ego-mind to regain control over us by taking us back to the old patterns of thoughts, emotions and activities. With higher awareness, insight and practising a 100 per cent experience of the present, we will be able to liberate the present moment, which is life, from the grip of the ego-mind and experience the state of awakening.

Check whether your present moment is liberated from the ego-mind.

　i. Are you mentally resisting change, practising meditation and other reprogramming methods?
　ii. Are you aware of the thoughts, especially the addictive incessant ones? Can you observe those and create gaps in between thoughts?
　iii. Are you able to experience the present moment in isolation, which is whole, and find happiness in it?
　iv. Being aware that past and future are non-existent and illusions, are you free from all worries of the past and anxieties about the future?
　v. Are you free from unwanted thoughts and any shred of negative emotional reaction?
　vi. Do you treat others as equals?
　vii. Do you respond rationally to all life situations based on the principle of 'nothing more, nothing less'?

This check and feedback will help us become aware of the extent of transformation and awakening we have achieved or are yet to achieve and commit ourselves to continue practising the reprogramming methods, meditation and move further towards the state of awakening.

Higher Purpose

We have seen that the ultimate goal of our life is to evolve spiritually, realize that we are spiritual beings with human experiences. It is also our higher purpose in life that the higher awareness is disseminated to people around the world through all our thoughts, feelings, actions and experiences. When our actions are rooted in the spiritual dimension's presence, they will be of a higher quality and a spiritual experience manifesting our beingness—people around us will experience it, and it will also help them evolve spiritually.

Manifestation of Consciousness

An awakened life means the manifestation of consciousness through human experiences. We cannot seek and find it like an object because we exist within it—we are it. Everything happens and is experienced within consciousness. Its basic nature is deep joy, peace and love; in the absence of its blockade, consciousness emerges as awareness and experience, in short intervals initially, and we perceive things in the spiritual dimension, the presence, just like brightness in the daytime without clouds. This is true happiness, the real joy felt from the experience of beingness. It is a timeless dimension, the presence. Even full attention and experience of little things bring us the presence and experience of this dimension.

So, all experiences happen in consciousness, and it is the experience of the real you. We cannot fully explain it with language and understand it intellectually or interpret it with our logical minds. It is beyond name, it is formless. You can be aware of it, access and experience it only in the now. Our ultimate goal in life is to become aware of this truth that we are consciousness and remove blockades of its experience so that it is realized, experienced and manifested automatically through human experiences—a state of awakening.

A few people are able to become awakened through certain rare life situations, like a sudden loss of dear ones, life-threatening accidents or extreme physical endurance. Awakening means the experience of complete liberation of our life or the present moment from the control of the ego-mind or past and future.

So to put it in the words of Einstein, 'The true value of a human being can be found in the degree to which he has attained liberation from self.' Here, self is to be seen as the ego-mind.

Now, We Have an Option

We have seen that as the ego-mind drove it, our life had been addicted to conflicts and pain, and we had little room for free will. With the higher awareness and insight we achieved, now we have an option—we can observe and become aware of our thoughts and emotional patterns and regulate them. This is a great achievement in the process of mind engineering and a journey towards awakening. We are also aware of the addictive and compulsive emotional reaction patterns that we followed so far, which created all the conflicts and pain in life. Now, we should take responsibility for what we are thinking, feeling and doing, and have a higher awareness that 'I am responsible for what I am thinking, feeling and doing,' and 'I create my reality'.

Insight Keeps Us in the Present

It is unconscious to waste our precious life and fortunes by creating conflict, pain and poor health for ourselves and others. Now, we, who undertook the spiritual journey with the mind engineering process, have reached a state of higher awareness or insight. We are aware that before this wisdom, we were slaves of the ego-mind, and our lives had been fully driven by the ego-mind; now, we are able to observe all its tendencies and strategies. We are fully aware that the basic strategy of the ego-mind is to deny us the experience of the precious present moment. So, with mind engineering wisdom and its processes, we have developed a state of insight; we can observe and be aware of our thoughts, emotions and the cunning ego-mind's tendencies that deny us presence. If our insight is not active, it means the ego-mind has taken control of us tactfully. So with this insight, we should, as frequently as we can, ask ourselves, 'Where is my attention', and analyse whether our attention has been deflected or distracted from the present moment.

Mindsight is a unique faculty of a human being with which we can be aware of our own awareness (meta-awareness). As this is a non-physical faculty beyond sensory perceptions, we need to become aware of it, believe in it, visualize and experience it to keep it active and powerful. Visualize that the part of the energy field around the body or the aura above the head is brightened further, like a powerful lit bulb, and operates as the sixth sense.

With this insight, we can be aware of subtle things, like thoughts, emotions, ego-mind's compulsive or addictive tendencies, emotional reaction patterns, subtle energy within the body, visualize images of internal organs and be aware of our state of mind. We can close our eyes and visualize and experience them. This practice is more effective during meditation, which will further strengthen the insight. With this insight, we can pay selective attention to anything we want and be present and remain focussed on it. If you are not engaged in any activity, you can focus your attention on your breath and remain present—that is meditation in itself.

The Ready Reckoner

Having received the higher wisdom and awareness, and being aware of the goal of life and its road map, the following are the ready reckoners and check-points:

   i. Always keep the insight active and functioning.

ii. Be fully aware of your attention and selectively focus it on the desired activity or object or state. The thumb rule of paying attention is that it should be a 100 per cent and it should be in the now.
iii. Make the focussed human experience a spiritual experience.

The more you practice and experience this, the more effective and powerful it will be. Our sensory experiences will be deeper, and we will find all activities equivalent to spiritual experiences, and we will be fully in the present and awakened state. This is the power of mind engineering.

NOTES

Chapter 1: Resistance to Change

1. Dispenza, Joe, Dr, *You Are the Placebo: Making Your Mind Matter*, Hay House, 2014.
2. McMillan, Pamela J., et al., 'Chronic cortisol exposure promotes the development of a GABAergic phenotype in the primate hippocampus', *Journal of Neurochemistry*, Vol. 91, No. 4, 2004, pp. 843–51.
3. Joergensen, Anders, et al., 'Association between Urinary Excretion of Cortisol and Markers of Oxidatively Damaged DNA and RNA in Humans', *PLoS One*, Vol. 6, No. 6, 2011, https://bit.ly/3btAQsd. Accessed on 24 June 2022.
4. Church, Dawson, *Mind to Matter: The Astonishing Science of How Your Brain Creates Material Reality*, Hay House, 2018.
5. Blackburn, Elizabeth and Elissa Epel, *The Telomere Effect: A Revolutionary Approach to Living Younger, Healthier, Longer*, Orion Spring, 2018, p. 79.
6. Lipton, Bruce H., *The Honeymoon Effect: The Science of Creating Heaven on Earth*, Hay House, 2013.
7. Harris, Mathew A., et al., 'Personality Stability From Age 14 to Age 77 Years', *Psychology and Aging*, Vol. 31, No. 8, 2016.
8. Eliade, Mircea, *Yoga: Immortality and Freedom*, Pantheon Books, 1958.

Chapter 2: Introspection

1. Harari, Yuval Noah, *Sapiens: A Brief History of Humankind*, Vintage, 2011.
2. Hawking, Stephen and Leonard Mlodinow, *The Grand Design*, Bantam Books, 2010, p. 153.
3. Hawking, Stephen and Leonard Mlodinow, 'Why God Did Not Create the Universe', *The Wall Street Journal*, 3 September 2010, https://on.wsj.com/3Oi5PFZ. Accessed on 22 June 2022.
4. Tolle, Eckhart, *A New Earth: Awakening to Your Life's Purpose*, Penguin, 2006, p. 11.
5. Kiecolt-Glaser, Janice K., et al., 'Emotions, Morbidity, and Mortality: New Perspectives from Psychoneuroimmunology', *Annual Review of Psychology*, Vol. 53, 2002, pp. 83–107.
6. Wu, Ming, et al., 'Interaction between Ras (V12) and scribbled clones induces tumour growth and invasion', *Nature*, Vol. 463, No. 7280, 2010, pp. 545–8.
7. Sloan, Erica K., et al., 'The Sympathetic Nervous System Induces a Metastatic Switch in Primary Breast Cancer', *Cancer Research*, Vol. 70, No. 18, 2010, https://bit.ly/3z9Kc5V. Accessed on 2 June 2022.
8. Sastry, Konduru S.R., et al., 'Epinephrine Protects Cancer Cells from Apoptosis via Activation of cAMP-dependent Protein Kinase and BAD Phosphorylation', *Journal of Biological Chemistry*, Vol. 282, No. 19, 2007, https://bit.ly/3x6gspg. Accessed on 2 June 2022.
9. Roy, Sashwati, et al., Wound site neutrophil transcriptome in response to psychological stress in young men', *Gene Expression*, Vol. 12, No. 4–6, 2005, pp. 273–87.
10. Barefoot, J.C., et al., 'Hostility, CHD incidence, and total mortality: a 25-year follow-up study of 255 physicians', *Psychosomatic Medicine*, Vol. 45, No. 1, 1983, pp. 59–63.
11. Berk, Lee S., et al., 'Neuroendocrine and Stress Hormone Changes

During Mirthful Laughter', *The American Journal of Medical Sciences*, Vol. 298, No. 6, 1989, pp. 390–6.

12 Park, Soyoung Q., et al., 'A neural link between generosity and happiness', *Nature Communications*, Vol. 8, No. 15964, 2017.

13 Kotler, Steven and Jamie Wheal, *Stealing Fire: How Silicon Valley, the Navy SEALs and Maverick Scientists Are Revolutionizing the Way We Live and Work*, HarperCollins, 2017.

14 Baumgartner, Thomas, et al., 'Oxytocin shapes the neural circuitry of trust and trust adaptation in humans', *Neuron*, Vol. 58, No. 4, 2008, pp. 639–50.

15 Geesink, Hans J.H. and Dirk K.F. Meijer, 'Quantum Wave Information of Life Revealed: An Algorithm for Electromagnetic Frequencies that Create Stability of Biological Order, With Implications for Brain Function and Consciousness', *NeuroQuantology*, Vol. 14, No. 1, 2016.

16 Giltay, Erik, et al., 'Dispositional optimism and all-cause and cardiovascular mortality in a prospective cohort of elderly Dutch men and women', *ACC Current Journal Review*, Vol. 14, No. 2, 2004; Diener, Ed and Micaela Y. Chan, 'Happy People Live Longer: Subjective Well-Being Contributes to Health and Longevity', *Applied Psychology: Health and Well-Being*, Vol. 3, No. 1, 2011.

17 Maruta, Toshihiko, et al., 'Optimism-pessimism assessed in the 1960s and self-reported health status 30 years later', *Mayo Clinic Proceedings*, Vol. 77, No. 8, 2002, pp. 748–53.

18 Siegler, Ilene C., et al., ' Patterns of change in hostility from college to midlife in the UNC Alumni Heart Study predict high-risk status', *Psychosomatic Medicine*, Vol. 65, No. 5, 2003, pp. 738–45.

19 Zahl, Per-Henrik, et al., 'The Natural History of Invasive Breast Cancers Detected by Screening Mammography', *Archives of Internal Medicine*, Vol. 168, No. 21, 2008 pp. 2311–6.

20 O'Regan, Brendan and Carlyle Hirshberg, *Spontaneous Remission: An Annotated Bibliography*, Institute of Noetic Sciences, 1993.

21 Berk, L.S., et al., 'Neuroendocrine and Stress Hormone Changes During Mirthful Laughter', *The American Journal of the Medical Sciences*, Vol. 298, No. 6, 1989, pp. 390–6.
22 Fredrickson, Barbara L. and Robert W. Levenson, 'Positive Emotions Speed Recovery from the Cardiovascular Sequelae of Negative Emotions', *Cognition and Emotion*, Vol. 12, No. 2, 1998, pp. 191–220.
23 Becker, D.M., et al., 'General Well-Being is Strongly Protective Against Future Coronary Heart Disease Events in an Apparently Healthy High-Risk Population', Abstract #103966, presented at American Heart Association Scientific Sessions, Anaheim, CA, 12 November 2001.
24 Dusek, Jeffery A. et al., 'Genomic Counter-Stress Changes Induced by the Relaxation Response', *Plos One*, Vol. 3, No. 7, 2008, pp. e2576.
25 Church, Dawson, *Mind to Matter: The Astonishing Science of How Your Brain Creates Material Reality*, Hay House, 2018.

Chapter 3: Basic Questions and the Goal of Life

1 Kahneman, Daniel and Angus Deaton, 'High income improves evaluation of life but not emotional well-being', *Proceedings of the National Academy of Sciences*, Vol. 107, No. 38, 2010, pp. 16489–93.
2 Tolle, Eckhart, *The Power of Now: A Guide to Spiritual Enlightenment*, Hodder and Stoughton, 2001, p. 68.
3 Thum, Myrko, 'What is the Present Moment?' 31 August 2018, https://bit.ly/39JhvTb. Accessed on 22 June 2022.
4 Lewis, C.S., *Surprised by Joy: The Shape of My Early Life*, Faded Page (Kindle Edition), 2020, p. 169.
5 Tolle, Eckhart, *A New Earth: Awakening to Your Life's Purpose*, Penguin Life, 2005, p. 166.

Chapter 5: Mind Engineering Model of Mind and Consciousness

1. Newberg, Andrew, et al., *Why God Won't Go Away: Brain Science and the Biology of Belief*, Ballantine Books, 2002.
2. Dispenza, Joe, Dr, *You Are the Placebo: Making Your Mind Matter*, Hay House, 2014.
3. Lipton, Bruce H., *The Honeymoon Effect: The Science of Creating Heaven on Earth*, Hay House, 2013.
4. Nørretranders, Tor, *The User Illusion: Cutting Consciousness Down to Size*, Penguin Books, New York, 1999.
5. Grinberg-Zylberbaum, J., et al., 'The Einstein-Podolsky-Rosen Paradox in the Brain: The Transferred Potential', *Physics Essays*, Vol. 7, No. 4, 1994.
6. Standish, Leanna J., et al., 'Electroencephalographic evidence of correlated event-related signals between the brains of spatially and sensory isolated human subjects', *Journal of Alternative and Complementary Medicine*, Vol. 10, No. 2, 2004, pp. 307–14.
7. Mc Taggart, Lynne, *The Intention Experiment: Using Your Thoughts to Change Your Life and the World*, HarperCollins, 2008, pp. 62–64.
8. Capra, Fritjof, *The Tao of Physics*, Shambhala Publications, 1991, p. 142.
9. Church, Dawson, *The Genie in Your Genes: Epigenetic Medicine and the New Biology of Intention*, Elite Books, 2007, p. 32.
10. James, William, *The Varieties of Religious Experience: A Study in Human Nature*, Fount, 1971, p. 374.
11. Skirry, Justin, Dr, *Descartes and the Metaphysics of Human Nature: 6 (Continuum Studies in Philosophy)*, Continuum International, 2006.
12. Miller, George Armitage, *Psychology: The Science of Mental Life*, Harper & Row, 1962.
13. Chalmers, David J., *The Conscious Mind: In Search of a Fundamental Theory*, Oxford University Press, 1996.

14. Damasio, Antonio R., *The Feeling of What Happens: Body and Emotion in the Making of Consciousness*, Harcourt, Brace & Co, 1999.
15. Pinker, Steven, *How the Mind Works*, W.W. Norton & Company, New York, 1997.
16. Pinker, Steven, 'How to think about the mind', *Newsweek*, 27 September 2004, https://bit.ly/3OudQr4. Accessed on 22 June 2022.
17. Parnia, Sam, Dr, et al., 'Results of world's largest Near Death Experiences study published', University of Southampton, 7 October 2014, https://bit.ly/2BkArnH. Accessed on 22 June 2022.
18. Myers, Frederic W.H., *Human Personality and Its Survival of Bodily Death Vol. 2 (1903)*, Kessinger Publishing, 2003.
19. Sheldrake, Rupert, *A New Science of Life: The Hypothesis of Morphic Resonance*, Park Street Press, 1981.
20. Penrose, Roger, *The Emperor's New Mind*, Oxford University Press, 1989.
21. Goswami, Amit, *Physics of the Soul: The Quantum Book of Living, Dying, Reincarnation, and Immortality*, Hampton Roads, 2001.
22. Radin, Dean, *The Conscious Universe: The Scientific Truth of Psychic Phenomena*, Harper Collins, 1997.
23. Sheldrake, Rupert, *A New Science of Life: The Hypothesis of Morphic Resonance*, Park Street Press, 1981.
24. Thomas, Lewis, *The Medusa and the Snail: More Notes of a Biology Watcher*, The Viking Press, 1979.
25. Rhine, Louisa E., 'Psychological Processes in ESP Experiences Part I. Waking Experiences', *The Journal of Parapsychology*, Vol. 26, No. 2, 1962, p. 88.
26. Rhine, Louisa E., 'Hallucinatory experiences and psychosomatic psi', *The Journal of Parapsychology*, Vol. 31, No. 2, 1967, pp. 111–34.
27. Stevenson, Ian, *Telepathic Impressions: A Review and Report of 35 New Cases*, University Press of Virginia, 1970.
28. Price, H.H, '[Review of] The Imprisoned Splendour, by R.C.

Johnson', *The Journal of Parapsychology*, Vol. 18, 1954, pp. 51–64.
29 Broad, C.D., *Religion, Philosophy and Psychical Research: Selected Essays*, Harcourt, Brace & Co, 1953.
30 James, William, *The Varieties of Religious Experience*, Mentor, 1958.
31 Bucke, Richard Maurice, *Cosmic Consciousness: A Study in the Evolution of the Human Mind*, Dutton, New York, 1969.
32 Russell, Bertrand, *Mysticism and Logic and Other Essays*, Longman, Green and Co., 1918.
33 James, William, *The Varieties of Religious Experience*, Mentor, 1958.
34 Stace, W.T., *Mysticism and Philosophy*, Oxford University Press, New York, 1987.
35 Eckhart, Meister, et al., *The Essential Sermons, Commentaries, Treatises, and Defense*, Paulist Press, New York, 1981.
36 Stace, W.T., *Mysticism and Philosophy*, Oxford University Press, New York, 1987.
37 Prabhavananda, Swami and Frederick Manchester, *The Upanishads: Breath of the Eternal*, New American Library, New York, 1957.
38 Koestler, Arthur, *The Invisible Writing*, Beacon Press, Boston, 1954.
39 Ibid.
40 Rabin, J. and J.L. Saver, 'The neural substrates of religious experience', *The Journal of Neuropsychiatry and Clinical Neuroscience*, Vol. 9, No. 3, 1997, pp. 498–510.
41 Gastaut, Henri, 'Fyodor Mikhailovitch Dostoevsky's Involuntary Contribution to the Symptomatology and Prognosis of Epilepsy, *Epilepsia*, Vol. 19, No. 2, pp. 186–201.
42 Thurston, H., 'The phenomena of stigmatization', *Proceedings of the Society for Physical Research*, Vol. 32, 1992, pp. 179–208.
43 Penfield, W. and Perot, P., 'The Brain's Records of Auditory and Visual Experience. Final Summary and Discussion', *Brain: A Journal of Neurology*, Vol. 86, 1963, pp. 595–696.
44 Halgren, E., et al., 'Mental phenomena evoked by electrical stimulation of the human hippocampal formation and amygdala',

Brain: A Journal of Neurology, Vol. 101, No. 1, 1978, pp. 83–117; Halgren, E., 'Mental phenomena induced by stimulation in the limbic system', *Human Neurobiology*, Vol. 1, No. 4, 1982, pp. 251–60; Gloor, P., et al., 'The role of the limbic system in experiential phenomena of temporal lobe epilepsy', *Annals of Neurology*, Vol. 12, No. 2, 1982, pp. 129–44; Gloor, P., 'Experiential phenomena of temporal lobe epilepsy. Facts and hypotheses', *Brain: A Journal of Neurology*, Vol. 113, 1990, pp. 1673–94.

45 Freud, Sigmund, *Civilization and Its Discontents*, W.W. Norton & Company, New York, 1961.

46 Neumann, E., 'Mystical Man', *The Mysteries: Papers from the Eranos Yearbooks*, Joseph Campbell (ed.), Princeton University Press, 1979.

47 Broad, C.D., *Religion, Philosophy and Physical Research*, Harcourt, Brace & Co, New York, 1953.

48 Foster, Genevieve W., *The World Was Flooded with Light: A Mystical Experience Remembered*, University of Pittsburgh Press, 1985.

49 Kirlian, S.D. and V.K. Kirlian, 'Photography and visual observation by means of high frequency currents', *Journal of Applied Photographic Engineering*, Vol. 6, 1964, pp. 397–403.

50 Korotkov, K., *Human Energy Field: Study with GDV Bioelectrography*, Backbone Publishing, New Jersey, 2002; Korotkov, K., *Aura and Consciousness: New Stage of Scientific Understanding*, St Petersburg division of the Russian Ministry of Culture, State Publishing Unit 'Kultura', 1999.

51 Calaprice, A. (ed.), *Dear Professor Einstein: Albert Einstein's Letters to and from Children*, Prometheus Books, New York, 2002.

52 Moody, Raymond A., *Life After Life*, Mockingbird Books, 1975.

53 Moorjani, Anita, *Dying to be Me: My Journey from Cancer, to Near Death, to True Healing*, Hay House, 2012.

54 Alexander, Eben, Dr, *Proof of Heaven: A Neurosurgeon's Journey Into the Afterlife*, Piatkus, 2012.

55 Ring, Kenneth and Sharon Cooper, *Mindsight: Near-Death and Out-Of-Body Experiences in the Blind*, iUniverse, 2008.
56 Neal, Matt, 'Sir John Eccles, Victoria's Nobel Prize-winning scientist who was marginalised in his search for the soul', ABC News, 13 August 2018, https://ab.co/3bjSSgm. Accessed on 22 June 2022.
57 Popp, Fritz-Albert, 'About the Coherence of Biophotons', International Institute of Biophysics, https://bit.ly/3NdKWKC. Accessed on 22 June 2022.
58 McTaggart, Lynne, *The Field: The Quest for the Secret Force of the Universe*, Element, 2003.
59 Clarke, A.C., 'When will the real space age being?' *Ad Astra*, May-June 1996, pp. 13–15.
60 Aspect, Alain, et al., 'Experimental tests of Bell's inequalities using time-varying analyzers', *Physical Review Letters*, Vol. 49, 1982, No. 25, pp. 1804–7.
61 Sheldrake, Rupert, *Seven Experiments That Could Change the World: A Do-it-yourself Guide to Revolutionary Science*, Park Street Press, 2002.
62 Michelson, Albert A. and Edward W. Morley, 'On the relative motion of the Earth and the luminiferous ether', *The American Journal of Science*, Vol. s3-34, No. 203, 1887, pp. 333–45.
63 Planck, Max, *Scientific Autobiography, and Other Papers*, Williams and Norgate, 1950.
64 Capra, F., *The Tao of Physics*, Shambhala Publications, 1975.
65 Bucke, Richard Maurice, *Cosmic Consciousness: A Study in the Evolution of the Human Mind*, Dutton, New York, 1969.
66 Emery, David, 'Did Albert Einstein Say "We Are Slowed-Down Sound and Light Waves"?' Snopes, 5 June 2019, https://bit.ly/2LqheWB. Accessed on 22 June 2022.
67 Tonneau, F., 'Consciousness Outside the Head', *Behaviour and Philosophy*, Vol. 32, No. 1, 2001, pp. 97–123.
68 Zohar, Danah, *The Quantum Self*, Flamingo, London, 1991.

69 Mc Taggart, Lynne, *The Field: The Quest for the Secret Force of the Universe*, Element, 2003.
70 Hoss, R. 'Consciousness After the Body Dies', Presentation at the International Association for the study of Dreams, 12 June 2016, Kerkrade, Netherlands.
71 'Spiritual quotes of Shankara', https://bit.ly/3zSjDTl. Accessed on 22 June 2022.

Chapter 6: Consciousness and Presence

1 Bradt, Steve, 'Wandering mind not a happy mind', *The Harvard Gazette*, 11 November 2010, https://bit.ly/3zRKhf7. Accessed on 22 June 2022.

Chapter 7: Origin, Growth and Operation of the Ego-Mind

1 Kinsella, Michael T. and Catherine Monk, 'Impact of Maternal Stress, Depression & Anxiety on Fetal Neurobehavioral Development', *Clinical Obstetrics and Gynecology*, Vol. 52, No. 3, 2009, pp. 425–40.
2 Lipton, Bruce H., *The Honeymoon Effect: The Science of Creating Heaven on Earth*, Hay House, 2014, pp. 94.
3 Roy, Sashwati, et al., 'Wound site neutrophil transcriptome in response to psychological stress in young men', *Gene Expression*, Vol.12, No. 4–6, 2005, pp. 273–87.

Chapter 8: Freedom from Emotional Reaction and Pain

1 James, Geoffrey, 'Science Says Your Brain is Hardwired to Be Happy (If You Know This Simple Trick)', Inc.com, https://bit.ly/3OBtcdi. Accessed on 23 June 2022.
2 Davidson, Richard J., 'Affective neuroscience and psychophysiology: toward a synthesis', *Psychophysiology*, Vol. 40, No. 5, 2003, pp. 655–65.

Chapter 9: Thoughts and Energy

1. Dispenza, Joe, Dr, *You Are the Placebo: Making Your Mind Matter*, Hay House, 2014.
2. Goleman, Daniel, et al., *Measuring the Immeasurable: The Scientific Case for Spirituality*, Sounds True, 2008, p. 196; H. Lipton, Bruce, and Steve Bhaerman, *Spontaneous Evolution: Our Positive Future and a Way to There from Here*, Hay House, 2009, p. 25.
3. Dispenza, Joe, Dr, *You Are the Placebo: Making Your Mind Matter*, Hay House, 2014, p. 51.
4. Peale, Norman, V., *The Power of Positive Thinking*, Prentice Hall, 1952.
5. Dispenza, Joe, Dr, *You Are the Placebo: Making Your Mind Matter*, Hay House, 2014, p. xii.
6. McCraty, Rollin, et al., 'Modulation of DNA Conformation by Heart-Focussed Intention', Heart Math Research Center, Institute of HeartMath, 2003, Publication No. 03–008.
7. Kramer, Adam D., et al., 'Experimental evidence of massive-scale emotional contagion through social networks', *Proceedings of the National Academy of Sciences of the United States of America*, Vol. 111, No. 24, 2014, pp. 8788–90.
8. Barsade, Sigal G., 'The Ripple Effect: Emotional Contagion and Its Influence on Group Behaviour', *Administrative Science Quarterly*, Vol. 47, No. 4, 2002, pp. 644–75.
9. Fowler, James H. and Nicholas A. Christakis, 'Dynamic spread of happiness in a large social network: Longitudinal analysis over 20 years in the Framingham Heart Study', *British Medical Journal*, Vol. 337, 2008.
10. 'Capital Crime: Rape Tripled, Kidnapping of Women Doubled in Delhi in Last 10 Years, Says Police Data', News 18, 31 March 2022, https://bit.ly/3n5OBQa. Accessed on 22 June 2022.
11. Siegler, Irene C., et al., 'Patterns of change in hostility from college

to midlife in the UNC Alumni Heart Study predict high-risk status', *Psychosomatic Medicine*, Vol. 65, No. 5, 2003, pp. 738–45.
12 Barefoot, J.C., et al., 'Hostility, CHD incidence, and total mortality: A 25-year follow-up study of 255 physicians', *Psychosomatic Medicine*, Vol. 45, No. 1, 1983, pp. 59–63.
13. Kandel E.R., 'A new intellectual framework for psychiatry', *The American Journal of Psychiatry*, Vol. 155, No. 4, 1998, pp. 457–69.
14 Pert, Candance B. Pert, *Molecules of Emotion*, Scribner, New York, 2003.
15 Maruta, Toshihiko, et al., 'Optimism-pessimism assessed in the 1960s and self-reported health status 30 years later', *Mayo Clinic Proceedings*, Vol. 77, No. 8, 2002, pp. 748–53.
16 Maruta, Toshihiko, et al., 'Optimists vs Pessimists: Survival Rate Among Medical Patients Over a 30-Year Period', *Mayo Clinic Proceedings*, Vol. 75, No. 2, 2000, pp. 140-3.
17 Swaminathan, Nikhil, 'Why Does the Brain Need So Much Power?' Scientific American, 29 April 2008, https://bit.ly/3ybGwjj. Accessed on 22 June 2022.
18 Church, Dawson, *Mind to Matter: The Astonishing Science of How Your Brain Creates Material Reality*, Hay House, 2018, p. 111.
19 Taylor, Jill Bolte, *My Stroke of Insight: A Brain Scientist's Personal Journey*, Penguin Books, 2009, p. 18.
20 Sinclair, David A., *Lifespan : Why We Age – and Why We Don't Have To*, Thorsons, 2019.

Chapter 10: Why is Meditation Essential?

1 'National Survey Reveals Increased Use of Yoga, Meditation, and Chiropractic Care Among U.S. Adults', National Center for Complementary and Integrative Health, https://bit.ly/3HLPnLW. Accessed on 22 June 2022.
2 Thera, Nyanaponika, *The Power of Mindfulness*, Buddhist Publication Society, 2014.

3   Raichle, Marcus E. et al., 'A default mode of brain function', *Proceedings of the National Academy of Sciences of the United States of America*, Vol. 98, No. 2, 2001, pp. 676–82, https://bit.ly/3NZdpFd. Accessed on 16 June 2022.

4   R. Andrews-Hanna, Jesscia, 'The Brain's Default Network and its Adaptive Role in Internal Mentation', *The Neuroscientist*, Vol. 18, No. 3, 2012, pp. 251–70.

5   Church, Dawson, *Mind to Matter: The Astonishing Science of How Your Brain Creates Material Reality*, Hay House, 2018, p. 109.

6   Rosenkranz, Melissa A. et al., 'Reduced stress and inflammatory responsiveness in experienced meditators to a matched healthy control group', *Psychonueroimmunology*, Vol. 68, 2016, 117–25.

7   Benson, Herbert, *The Relaxation Response*, William Morrow, New York, 1975.

8   Wallace, B. Alan, *The Attention Revolution: Unlocking the Power of the Focussed Mind*, Wisdom Publications, Somerville, 2006.

9   Miura, Isshu and Ruth Fuller Sasaki, *The Zen Koan: Its History and Use in Rinzai Zen*, Harcourt, Brace & Co, New York, 1965, p. xi.

10 Kral, Tammi R.A., et al., 'Impact of short- and long-term mindfulness meditation training on amygdala reactivity to emotional stimuli,' *Neuroimage*, Vol. 181, 2018, pp. 301–13.

11 Goleman, Daniel J., and Gary E. Schwartz, 'Meditation as an Intervention in stress reactivity', *Journal of Consulting and Clinical Psychology*, Vol. 44, No. 3, 1976, pp. 456–66.

12 Kabat-Zinn, Jon, 'Mindfulness-Based Interventions in Context: Past, Present and Future,' *Clinical Psychology Science and Practice*, Vol. 10, No. 2, 2003, p. 145.

13 Kandel, Eric R., 'A New Intellectual Framework for Psychiatry', *American Journal of Psychiatry*, Vol. 155, No. 4, 1998, pp. 457–69.

14 Luders, Eileen et al., 'Estimating brain age using high-resolution pattern recognition: Younger brains in long-term meditation practitioners', *Neuroimage*, Vol. 134, 2016.

15 'Experienced meditators have brains that are physically 7 years younger than non-meditators', Research Digest, 15 April 2016, https://bit.ly/3OPdAmT. Accessed on 22 June 2022.
16 Goleman, Daniel and Richard Davidson, *The Science of Meditation: How to Change Your Brain, Mind and Body*, Penguin Life, 2017.
17 Crick, F., *The Astonishing Hypothesis: The Scientific Search for the Soul*, Simon & Schuster, New York, 1994.
18 Goleman, Daniel and Richard Davidson, *The Science of Meditation: How to Change Your Brain, Mind and Body*, Penguin Life, 2017.
19 Schwartz, Jeffrey M. and Sharon Begley, *The Mind and the Brain: Neuroplasticity and the Power of Mental Force*, Springer Science & Business Media, New York, 2009.
20 Austin, James H., *Zen and the Brain: Toward an Understanding of Meditation and Consciousness*, MIT Press, Cambridge, 1999.
21 Ibid.
22 Goldin, Philippe R. and James J. Gross, 'Effects of Mindfulness-Based Stress Reduction (MBSR) on Emotion Regulation in Social Anxiety Disorder', *Emotion*, Vol. 10, No. 1, 2010, pp. 83–91; Wallace, Alan, *The Attention Revolution: Unlocking the Power of the Focussed Mind*, Wisdom Publications, 2006.
23 Beck, Charlotte Joko, *Nothing Special: Living Zen*, Harper Collins, New York, 1993, p. 168.
24 Jha, Amishi P. et al., 'Mindfulness training modifies subsystems of attention', *Cognitive, Affective and Behavioural Neuroscience*, Vol. 7, No. 2, 2007, pp. 109–19.
25 Gorman, Thomas E. and C. Shawn Green, 'Short-term mindfulness intervention reduces the negative attentional effects associated with heavy media multitasking', *Scientific Reports*, Vol. 6, 2016.
26 Mrazek, Michael D., et al., 'Mindfulness and mind wandering: finding convergence through opposing constructs', *Emotion*, Vol. 12, No. 3, 2012, 442–48.
27 Harris, Sam, *Waking Up: A Guide to Spirituality Without Religion*,

Simon & Schuster, New York, 2015, p. 144.
28 Cresswell, David, J., et al., 'Mindfulness-Based Stress Reduction training reduces loneliness and pro-inflammatory gene expression in older adults: a small randomized controlled trial', *Brain, Behaviour, and Immunity*, Vol. 26, No. 7, 2012, pp. 1095–101.
29 Schutte, Nicola, S. and John M. Malouff, 'A meta-analytic review of the effects of mindfulness meditation on telomerase activity', *Psychoneuroendocrinology*, Vol. 42, 2014, pp. 45–8.
30 Wielgosz, Joseph, et al., 'Long-term mindfulness training is associated with reliable differences in resting respiration rate', *Scientific Reports*, Vol. 6, 2016.
31 Lazar, Sara W. et al., 'Meditation experience is associated with increased cortical thickness', *Neuroreport*, Vol. 16, No. 17, 2005, pp. 1893–97.
32 Luders, Eileen et al., 'Estimating brain age using high-resolution pattern recognition: Younger brains in long-term meditation practitioners', *Neuroimage*, Vol. 134, 2016.
33 Segal, Zindel V., et al., *Mindfulness-Based Cognitive Therapy for Depression*, Guilford Press, New York, 2003; Teasdale, John D., et al., 'Prevention of relapse/recurrence in major depression by mindfulness-based cognitive therapy', *Journal of Consulting and Clinical Psychology*, Vol. 68, No. 4, 2000, pp. 615–23.

Chapter 11: Healing Power of the Mind

1 'The Effects of Stress on Your Body', WebMD, 8 December 2021, https://wb.md/3tURebj. Accessed on 22 June 2022.
2 Nijhout, H.F., 'Metaphors and the role of genes in development', *Bioessays*, Vol. 12, No. 9, 1990, pp. 441–46.
3 Willett, Walter C., 'Balancing life-style and genomics research for disease prevention', *Science*, Vol. 296, No. 5568, 2002, pp. 695–98.
4 Segerstrom, Suzanne C. and Gregory E. Miller, 'Psychological stress and the human immune system: a meta-analytic study

of 30 years of inquiry', *Psychological Bulletin*, Vol. 130, No. 4, 2004, pp. 601–30; Kopp, Mária S. and János Réthelyi, 'Where psychology meets physiology: chronic stress and premature mortality—The Central-Eastern European health paradox', *Brain Research Bulletin*, Vol. 62, No. 5, 2004, pp. 351–67; McEwen, B.S. and T. Seeman, 'Protective and damaging effects of mediators of stress. Elaborating and testing the concepts of allostasis and allostatic load', *Annals of the New York Academy of Sciences*, Vol. 896, 1999, pp. 30–47.

5   Rossi, E.L., *The Psychobiology of Gene Expression: Neuroscience and Neurogenesis in Hypnosis and the Healing Arts*, W. W. Norton and Company, 2002, p. 50.

6   McClare, C.W., 'Resonance in Bioenergetics', *Annals of the New York Academy of Sciences*, Vol. 227, 1974, pp. 74–97.

7   Ibid.

8   Cousins, N. 'Anatomy of an illness (as perceived by the patient)', *New England Journal of Medicine*, Vol. 295, No. 26, 1976, pp. 1458–63.

9   Tello, Monique, 'A positive mindset can help your heart', Harvard Health Publishing, 6 March 2019, https://bit.ly/2U1OtFk. Accessed on 22 June 2022.

10 Fuente-Fernández, Raúl de la, et al., 'Expectation and Dopamine Release: Mechanism of the Placebo Effect in Parkinson's Disease', *Science*, Vol. 293, No. 5532, 2001, pp. 1164–6.

11 Wahlestedt, Martin, et al., 'Clonal reversal of aging-associated stem cell lineage bias via a pluripotent intermediate', *Nature Communications*, Vol. 8, No. 14533, 2017.

12 Bianconi, Eva, et al., 'An estimation of the number of cells in the human body', *Annals of Human Biology*, Vol. 40, No. 6, 2013, pp. 463–71.

13 Zahl, Per-Henrik, et al., 'The Natural History of Invasive Breast Cancers Detected by Screening Mammography', *Archives of Internal Medicine*, Vol. 168, No. 21, 2008, pp. 2311–16.

14 Krikorian, J.G., et al., 'Spontaneous regression of non-Hodgkin's lymphoma: A report of nine cases', *Cancer*, Vol. 46, No. 9, 1980, pp. 2093–99.
15 O'Regan, B. and C. Hirshberg C, *Spontaneous remission: An annotated bibliography*, Institute of Noetic Sciences, 1993.
16 Levine, J.D., et al., 'The mechanism of placebo analgesia', *Lancet*, Vol. 2N no. 8091, 1978, pp. 654–57; Levine, J.D., et al., 'The narcotic antagonist naloxone enhances clinical pain', *Nature*, Vol. 272, No. 5656, 1978, pp. 826–27.
17 'Miraculous healing with Mind Engineering', 7 August 2021, https://bit.ly/3ycJd3W. Accessed on 22 June 2022.
18 Achterberg, Jeanne, *Imagery in Healing: Shamanism and Modern Medicine*, Shambhala Publications, 2002.
19 Kandel, Eric R., *In Search of Memory: The Emergence of a New Science of Mind*, W.W. Norton & Company & Company, 2006.
20 Segerstrom, Suzanne C. and Gregory E. Miller, 'Psychological stress and the human immune system: a meta-analytic study of 30 years of inquiry', *Psychological Bulletin*, Vol. 130, No. 4, 2004, pp. 601–30; S. Kopp, Mária and János Réthelyi, 'Where psychology meets physiology: chronic stress and premature mortality–The Central-Eastern European health paradox', *Brain Research Bulletin*, Vol. 62, No. 5, 2004, pp. 351–67; McEwen, B.S. and T. Seeman, 'Protective and damaging effects of meditators of stress. Elaborating and testing the concepts of allostasis and allostatic load', *Annals of the New York Academy of Sciences*, Vol. 896, 1999, pp. 30–47.
21 Richardson, K., *The Making of Intelligence*, Columbia University Press, 2000.
22 Rossi, Earnest Lawrence, *The Psychobiology of Gene Expression: Neuroscience and Neurogenesis in Hypnosis and the Healing Arts*, W.W. Norton & Company, 2002, p. 9.
23 Dispenza, Joe, Dr, *You Are the Placebo: Making Your Mind Matter*, Hay House, 2014, p. 86.

24 Lipton, Bruce, *The Biology of Belief: Unleashing the Power of Consciousness, Matter & Miracle*, Hay House UK, 2011.

25 Amanzio, M., and F. Benedetti, 'Neuropharmacological dissection of placebo analgesia: Expectation–activated opioid systems versus conditioning activated specific subsystems', *Journal of Neuroscience*, Vol. 19, No. 1, 1999, pp. 484–94.

26 Kirsch, Irving, and Guy Sapirstein, 'Listening to Prozac but hearing placebo: A meta-analysis of antidepressant medication', *Prevention and Treatment*, Vol. 1, No. 2, 1998.

27 Kirsch, Irving, et al., 'Initial severity and antidepressant benefits: a meta-analysis of data submitted to the Food and Drug Administration', *PLOS Medicine*, Vol. 5, No. 2, 2008, p. e45.

28 Thomas, L., 'Warts', *Human Nature*, Vol. 2, 1979, pp. 58–59.

29 Leuchter, Andrew F., et al., 'Changes in brain function of depressed subjects during treatment with placebo', *American Journal of Psychiatry*, Vol. 159, No. 1, 2002, pp. 122–29.

30 Fuente-Fernández, Raul de la, et al., 'Expectation and dopamine release: mechanism of the placebo effect in Parkinson's disease', *Science*, Vol. 293, No. 5532, 2001, pp. 1164–6.

31 Benson, H. and D.P. McCallie Jr, 'Angina pectoris and the placebo effect', *The New England Journal of Medicine*, Vol. 300, No. 25, 1979, pp. 1429–9.

32 Kirsch, Irving and Guy Saperstein, 'Listening to Prozac but hearing placebo: A meta-analysis of antidepressant medication', *Prevention and Treatment*, Vol. 1, No. 2, 1998.

33 Benedeti, Fabrizio, et al., 'Conscious expectation and unconscious conditioning in analgesic, motor, and hormonal placebo/nocebo responses', *The Journal of Neuroscience*, Vol. 25, No. 45, 2005, pp. 10390–402.

34 Bengston, W.F., *The Energy Cure: Unravelling the Mystery of Hands-On Healing*, Sounds True, 2010.

35 Green, Elmer E., et al., 'Autonomous Electrostatic Phenomena

in Exceptional Subjects', *Subtle Energies and Energy Medicine*, Vo. 2, No.3, 1993; Tiller, William A., et al., 'Towards Explaining Anomalously Large Body Voltage Surges on Exceptional Subjects. Part I: The Electrostatic Approximation', *Journal of Scientific Exploration*, Vol. 9, No. 3, 1995, pp. 331–50.

36 Tiller, William A., 'Subtle energies', *Science & Medicine*, Vol. 6, No. 3, 1999, pp. 28–33.

37 Creat, Katherine and Gary E. Schwartz, 'What Biophoton Images of Plants Can Tell Us About Biofields and Healing', *Journal of Scientific Exploration*, Vol. 19, No. 4, 2005, pp. 531–50.

38 McTaggart, Lynne, *The Intention Experiment: Use Your Thoughts to Change the World*, HarperCollins, 2008.

39 Eden, Donna, et al., *Energy medicine: Balancing Your Body's Energies for Optimal Health, Joy, and Vitality*, TarcherPerigee, 2008.

40 Dispenza, Joe, Dr, *You Are The Placebo: Making Your Mind Matter*, Hay House, 2014, p. xvii.

41 Targ, E., 'Evaluating distant healing: a research review', *Alternative Therapies in Health and Medicine*, Vol. 3, No. 6, 1997, pp. 74–8.

42 Hammerschlag, Richard, et al., 'Non-touch biofield therapy: a systematic review of human randomized controlled trials reporting use of only nonphysical contact treatment', *Journal of Alternative and Complementary Medicine*, Vol. 20, No. 12, 2014, pp. 881–92.

43 McTaggart, Lynne, *The Intention Experiment: Use Your Thoughts to Change the World*, HarperCollins, 2008.

44. Kirlian, S.D. and V.K. Kirlian, 'Photography and visual observation by means of high frequency currents', *Journal of Applied Photographic Engineering*, Vol. 6, 1964, pp. 397–403.

Chapter 12: Reprogramming of Subconscious Mind

1 Rothschild, Miriam, *The Rothschild Gardens*, Hamlyn, 2001.

2 LeDoux, Joseph E., 'Emotion Circuits in the Brain', *Annual Reviews of Neuroscience*, Vol. 23, 2000, pp. 155–84.

3   Stokes, Hilary and Kimberly Ward, *The Happy Map: Your Roadmap to the Habit of Happiness*, Bonsai Press, 2014.
4   Harris, Mathew A., et al., 'Personality stability from age 14 to age 77 years', *Psychology and Aging*, Vol. 31, No. 8, 2016.
5   Squire, Larry R. and E.R. Kandel, *Memory: From Mind to Molecules*, Scientific American Library, New York, 1999.
6   Taylor, Jill Bolte, *My Stroke of Insight*, Viking Press, 2008.
7   'Roger W. Sperry Nobel Lecture', The Nobel Prize, https://bit.ly/39uKry6. Accessed on 17 June 2022.
8   Raichle, Marcus E., et al., 'A default mode of brain function', *Proceedings of the National Academy of Sciences of the United States of America*, Vol. 98, No. 2, 2001, pp. 676–82.
9   Garrison, Kathleen A., et al., 'Effortless awareness: using real-time neurofeedback to investigate correlates of posterior cingulate cortex activity in meditators' self-report', *Frontiers in Human Neuroscience*, Vol. 7, No. 440, 2013, pp. 1–9.
10 'Now, rewire your brain in just 21 days!', *The Economic Times*, 8 February 2016, https://bit.ly/3O996Y6. Accessed on 22 June 2022.

Chapter 13: Why Is Practice Essential?

1   Crum, Alia J. and Ellen J. Langer, 'Mind-set matters: exercise and the placebo effect', *Psychological Science,* Vol. 18, No. 2, 2007, pp. 165–71.

Chapter 14: Accessing and Experiencing Awakening

1   Nørretranders, Tor, *The User Illusion: Cutting Consciousness Down to Size*, Penguin, New York, 1998.
2   Jamal, Alfea, '"I was determined", says Jyoti Kumari, the 15-year-old who cycled injured father across India', *Hindustan Times*, 28 May 2020, https://bit.ly/3ybcTPc. Accessed on 23 June 2022.
3   Teen Sisters Lift a 3,000lb Tractor to Rescue Their Father Who Was Pinned Underneath', *Daily Mail*, 10 April 2013.

4 Burleson, Katherine O. and Gary E Schwartz, 'Energy healing training and heart rate variability', *Journal of Alternative and Complementary Medicine*, Vol. 11, No. 3, 2005, pp. 391–3.
5 McTaggart, Lynne, *The Field: The Quest for the Secret Force of the Universe*, Element, 2003.

BIBLIOGRAPHY

Aspect, Alain, 'Bell's inequality test: more ideal than ever', *Nature*, Vol. 398, 1999, pp. 189–90.

Cooperstein, M. Allan, 'The Myths of Healing: summary of research into transpersonal healing experiences', *Journal of American Society for Psychical Research*, Vol. 86, No. 2, 1992, pp. 99–133.

Eccles, John C. and Karl Pooper, *The Self and Its Brain: An Argument for Interactionism*, Routledge, 1984.

Eccles, John Carew, *The Human Mystery*, Routledge, 1984.

Hamilton, Trever, *Immortal Longings: FWH Myers and the Victorian Search for Life After Death*, Andrews UK Limited, 2015.

Pop, Fritz Albert and Qiao Gu, *Recent Advances in Biophoton Research and Its Applications*, World Scientific, 1992.